French Ghosts, Russian Ni...
and America...

"A diverse and entertaining ... kling, honest, and emotional ... ...ny-fishing in Mexico, to the Icehotel in A... ...en, to Fellini's Rome. I got a peek into Julia Childs' world in Paris and Butch Cassidy's in Utah. I took language classes in China and ate in a French/Vietnamese restaurant in Hanoi. We went on foot, on buses, in taxis, on boats, on subways . . . to shacks and castles, temples and cemeteries. There are a lot of valuable examples here on how to travel alone while constantly connecting with others."
— Rita Golden Gelman, *Tales of a Female Nomad: Living at Large in the World*

"Urged on by a lively curiosity and a large dose of courage, Susan Spano introduces us to unusual destinations, often tempting and invariably interesting."
— Mary Taylor Simeti, *On Persephone's Island*

"Susan manages that most important travel writing feat: making you want to pack your bag, grab your passport, and go! I'm ready to jump on my bicycle and hit the backroads of County Clare or tie up my walking shoes and set foot on that coastal trail in France's Brittany. In the right car, I'd be happy to wind down Mulholland Highway as well ... although I'm not so sure about chasing speeding tickets with a Hummer in Arizona."
— Tony Wheeler, founder of the Lonely Planet series

"An easy-to-read travel writer"
— *Fodor's Travel*

Susan Spano has received three Lowell Thomas Awards from the Society of American Travel Writers

French Ghosts, Russian Nights, and American Outlaws

Susan Spano

ROARING FORTIES
PRESS

Roaring Forties Press
1053 Santa Fe Avenue
Berkeley, CA 94706

www.roaringfortiespress.com

Interior and cover design by Nigel Quinney.
Cover photograph: © iStockphoto.com/shaunl.
Author photograph by Susan Schiffer.

Library of Congress Cataloging-in-Publication Data
Spano, Susan.
  French ghosts, Russian nights, and American outlaws :
souvenirs of a professional vagabond / Susan Spano.
    pages cm
  ISBN 978-1-938901-24-9 (paperback : alkaline paper) -- ISBN
(invalid) 978-1-938901-25-6 (PDF) -- ISBN 978-1-938901-26-3
(ePub) -- ISBN
978-1-938901-27-0 (Kindle)
1. Spano, Susan--Travel. 2. Spano, Susan--Philosophy.
3. Voyages and travels. 4. Women travelers--Biography. 5.
Travel--Psychological
aspects. I. Title.
  G465.S668 2014
  910.4--dc23
                                    2014003609

To Sarah, may she travel far

"No manner of living would have interested me so much and so long and I will surely go on until I drop trying to see more of the world and what's happening in it."

— Martha Gellhorn,
Travels with Myself and Another

CONTENTS

Part 3: Souvenirs

ACKNOWLEDGEMENTS

I have been blessed in my editors, and twice blessed to be able to count them as friends—starting with Deirdre Greene, publisher of Roaring Forties Press. Her subtle editorial touch, pragmatism, and vision made this collection possible.

Generous, loyal Catharine Hamm of the *Los Angeles Times* gave me extraordinary freedom to tell travel stories I care about and to live abroad as a staff writer for the paper.

Janet Piorko launched me by picking my proposal to write a story for the travel section of the *New York Times* out of the slush pile and later by putting my name in the hat for the "Frugal Traveler" column. I couldn't have done it without her sharp intelligence and humor.

Nancy Newhouse, editor of the *New York Times* travel section during its heyday from 1989 to 2004, quite simply set the gold standard for what newspaper travel writing can be—literate, timely, ethical, and sophisticated.

❖ ❖

INTRODUCTION

As a travel writer for two of America's greatest newspapers—the *New York Times* and the *Los Angeles Times*—I could go almost anyplace I liked. All I had to do was write about it when I got back home.

I took unforgettable trips to Paris to chase literary ghosts; St. Petersburg, Russia, in the white depths of winter; the American West on the trail of Butch and Sundance; the seedy French Polynesian island of Huahine, where I was chased by a pack of wild dogs; and Venice in out-of-season splendor, with rainstorms flooding the Piazza San Marco. I took wild rides through Old Delhi in an auto-rickshaw, over the Yangtze River on a condemned cable car, and across the Andes in a shared taxi that reeked of gasoline. I hiked into lost canyons along Utah's Escalante River, through the jungles of Costa Rica, and across Morocco's Anti-Atlas Mountains, where some sneak thief stole my boots. The people I encountered are etched in my memory too, like the man in a laundromat in County Clare, Ireland, where I was biking in foul weather. "Ireland's a grand country," he told me. "Rain is the only fault in it."

I am not religious, but there were also moments of what I can only call spiritual rapture—when some part of me, some sap beneath the wood, responded to seeing the moon glow over a frozen lake above the Arctic Circle in Sweden or hearing the susurrus of chanting lamas at Potala Palace in Tibet.

I had bad trips, too: feeling sick to my stomach in Istanbul, trekking through the Libyan Sahara in a sandstorm, cold-camping in Alaska with a drunken guide. But though they're wretched at the time, bad trips make good stories. What better souvenir?

Only once, as I recall, did I find myself wanting to go home, and that was when I was 14, on a long bike ride through neighborhoods west of St. Louis, where I grew up. A quiet misfit in youth, I'd taken to riding away from our suburban tract home with no destination in mind, only a whim to see new things and figure out the lay of the land. In the heat of a midwestern summer I ended up at a gas station surrounded by cornfields, realizing that I'd gone too far to make it back home. So I asked the attendant to let me use his phone and called my mom. She didn't mind coming for me in our red Chevy station wagon. She was a geography teacher who took me on my first trip abroad a few years later—to Japan, where I found out it doesn't feel bad to be a foreigner, a stranger, a traveler.

I grew up knowing that if anything went wrong, no matter where I was, my mother and father would come for me. They are gone now, but I still wear that invisible shield.

With such a feeling, I could travel far and learn that the world is full of places nothing like St. Louis, each its own strange and marvelous confluence of history, culture, landscape, faith, and food.

When I say I have a love of place, I don't mean I love getting there. Twenty-hour plane rides are no fun. I don't love long lines, a suitcase full of dirty clothes, inglorious restrooms around the world. Nor do I mean that I have a need to plant my little flag on every continent, to be the first person to reach some mountaintop or remote village, to visit the hundred places some book tells us we must see before we die—I call that acquisitive travel. What I mean is that I love places, the feelings they evoke, the points of view they ask us to comprehend, the meanings they reveal.

Much has already been written about almost everywhere. Too much, perhaps. Of course, I read whatever I can get my hands on before embarking on a trip to avoid wasting time and making stupid mistakes. But I sometimes think it takes the adventure out of travel, ensuring that I will find only what I expect to find. So I add this book to the wide library of travel books with some trepidation, hoping just to describe some of the places I love and what happened to a girl on a bike who discovered that the world is full of stories waiting to be lived.

Part 1
UNFORGETTABLE

When people find out that I'm a travel writer, they often ask if I have a favorite place. They want itinerary advice; that's understandable.

But I cannot give it. I'm not a travel agent. I'm a traveler. I tend to think of travel as more about the trip than about the destination. And trips are delicate, changeable, precious operations, all too easily derailed. Encounters with even the most fabled destinations—say, Paris or Angkor Wat—are colored by such mundane factors as the weather and the speeding ticket you got along the way, and by purely subjective matters such as your health (to me Istanbul is a stomach bug), how you feel about your travel companion, and what's going on back home.

Soldier on, always. In travel, bad spells can be broken.

The trips I cherish most are the occasional ones that went precisely as planned, allowing me to deepen my understanding of people and places, exposing me to realities I never could have fathomed had I stayed home. But more and more, I recall surprise trips that didn't go as anticipated or that disappointed in certain ways. Martha Gellhorn wrote a whole book about horror trips. "We react alike to our tribulations," she said in *Travels with Myself and Another*. "Frayed and bitter at the time, proud afterwards. Nothing is better for self-esteem than survival."

The surprises are engraved in my memory—unforgettable, to use Nat King Cole's refrain.

THE EMERALD COAST

Walking alone along the footpath that rounds the Pointe du Grouin in northern Brittany, I met two Frenchmen headed the opposite way. We stopped and chatted about the glorious weather and how far I had to go before reaching Cancale, where I planned to eat oysters and spend the night. Just before going our separate ways, one of them commented on the fact that I was by myself and told me to be careful.

"What should I be careful of?" I asked seriously.

There was a pause, then the other man laughed and said, "Nothing. Absolutely nothing."

Caution is a good thing, as all travelers know. But trust is also called for sometimes. Without it, I'd never have gone walking 45 miles along the Emerald Coast of Brittany, from the walled seaport of St. Malo to Mont St. Michel, just across the River Couesnon in Normandy.

I knew that this was possible because France is crisscrossed by 25,000 miles of walking paths, called Grandes Randonnées, including the GR34, which follows the deeply indented Brittany coast for 360 miles. And I was planning a trip to London, putting me in striking distance of the path. So I booked passage on a ferry across the English Channel from Portsmouth to St. Malo, an 11-hour voyage.

While in in a bookshop just off Portobello Road in London, I chanced upon a copy of Alan Castle's *The Brittany Coastal Path*, which compares the merits of numerous seaside walking paths and finds the GR34 "far superior to any other with respect to the quality and variety of food on offer along the trail."

I should say so. Brittany is a chief producer of Muscadet wine, considered the perfect accompaniment to its exquisite oysters, carried daily to Versailles for the degustation of Louis XIV. I ate my first Brittany oyster many years ago and have never forgotten its pithy taste.

I could have made the trip in a rental car, available at the ferry terminal in St. Malo. Buses and trains take inland routes from there to Mont St. Michel too. But I wanted to walk because the GR34 sticks close to the scenic coast; walking is great exercise, meaning I could indulge at meals; and it's inexpensive.

Actually, the four-night trip would have been virtually free had I brought along camping gear, because the GR34 passes plenty of lovely spots to pitch a tent by quiet coves or atop lofty cliffs. But I don't like to camp by myself. So I trusted that I'd find rooms along the way in private *chambres d'hôtes* and modest one- or two-star hotels, which seemed likely because I'd be there before the busy summer season.

When I reached Portsmouth Harbor, I caught my first sight of the ferry—a sleek white vessel called *The Bretagne*, built in 1989 for Brittany Ferries, carrying automobiles, freight trucks, and up to 2,030 passengers. It looked like a cruise ship, with cinemas, a children's playroom, duty-free shops, a wine bar, a cafeteria, and cabins.

The sun was setting as we steamed out of the harbor, passing Portsmouth Naval Base, Admiral Nelson's *HMS Victory* berthed in the historic dock area, and the Isle of Wight. Standing by the stern rail, I noted the appropriateness of going to Brittany from Britain, which were connected physically before there was an English Channel and in other ways later. In the sixth century, Celts made the crossing, led by monks like the Welsh Maclow, who gave his name to St. Malo. Brittany was a battleground and prize coveted by both the French and English during the Hundred Years' War (1337–1453), and no one who sees its rugged coast can fail to remember the Allied invasion of France during World War II.

In fact, Allied bombs destroyed 80 percent of beautiful St.

Malo at the mouth of the River Rance. But you'd never know it when you arrive by ferry, slipping through the rocky islets scattered below its formidable granite walls, because after the war old St. Malo was rebuilt, stone by stone.

A modern city has grown up around it, and the sweeping beaches to the north and south are now lined by small, dignified hotels catering especially to English sun-seekers. But the 18th-century walled town remains an inviolate testament to the spirit of its residents, who resisted the French crown and the Duchy of Brittany, proclaiming St. Malo independent from 1590 to 1594. Its favorite native sons are the philosopher, Chateaubriand, buried on the little island of Grand-Bé, connected to the city by a sandy spit at low tide; the explorer, Jacques Cartier, whose statue stands atop the ramparts; and Robert Surcouf, a pirate who retired around 1800 as the wealthiest ship-owner in France.

On disembarkation, I shouldered my backpack and walked along a busy sailboat basin to the office of tourism just outside the northeast entrance to the walled city, called the Porte St. Vincent. There a nice woman sold me an excellent map of the Emerald Coast and, after much consultation, booked hotel rooms for me along the GR34. The first day I'd go an easy six miles to the hamlet of Rotheneuf and the Hotel Terminus; day two would be a 13.2-mile trek, with lots of ups and downs along the jagged coast, to the Hotel La Houle in Cancale; on the third day, the 11.8-mile walk would level out as I reached the polderland surrounding Mont St. Michel Bay and a *chambre d'hôte* in Cherrueix called L'Hebergement. From there, I'd head 13.8 miles to Mont St. Michel, tour the abbey, and catch a bus or train back to St. Malo—all on my last day.

It would have been nice to have a little extra time so that I could break up some of the longer segments of the walk and stay overnight at Mont St. Michel. But my schedule didn't allow it. Still, I refused to worry about what would happen if the weather turned foul or I got too tired to go on. I was in the hands of fate now.

Inside the walled city, there were reasons to believe that it would treat me gently, beginning with the steamed-mussel lunch special I had at one of the cafes on the Place Chateaubriand, and the sweet room I found on the third floor of the Hotel La Porte St. Pierre, its window looking out on the promenade atop the ramparts.

My one afternoon in St. Malo passed much too quickly. But I still managed to walk all the way around the ramparts and buy a blue-and-white striped French sailor's jersey. In the Municipal Museum on the Place Chateaubriand, I saw photos of the devastated city taken in August 1944, and on Bon Secours beach, I watched people walking out to Grand Bé and two little girls building a sandcastle that looked remarkably like St. Malo. Then I dressed for dinner at the pretty Restaurant de la Porte St. Pierre, where even the eel in the tank by the door looked happy. I ordered a half bottle of Muscadet, a seafood crepe, and *tarte tatin* for dessert.

The next morning, I ate a croissant and drank a big bowl of *café au lait* served downstairs at the hotel, put on my hiking boots, and walked out.

Actually, I could have gone barefoot for the first two or three miles, which traversed one long smashing beach after another on the way to the Pointe de la Varde near Rotheneuf. Halfway there, I wandered into an old hotel that houses a fancy spa called Thermes Marins de St. Malo, where I got a 30-minute algae wrap for 160 francs. It was an indulgence, but I had to consider my constitution, and the algae was local.

Later, standing at the verge of the clover-cloaked Pointe de la Varde, I imagined fitting the scalloped coasts of Cornwall and Brittany together like puzzle pieces, and caught my first sight of the red and white striped GR34 markings, which tend to be rather infrequent and subtly placed. Then it was on to Rotheneuf, where I settled into a room at the trim stone Hotel Terminus, walked half a mile to Jacques Cartier's home, Limoelou, saw rocks on the Pointe du Christ fantastically sculpted by a 19th-century hermit, sunbathed on the beach at Rotheneuf Harbor, and had an excellent *prix fixe* dinner at the Restaurant Limoelou in the center of the village. There the assorted cold seafood appetizer featured so many unusual mollusks that it looked like a shell collection, and the lotte came equitably coated in two sauces.

Castle's book offers two options for getting to the far side of Rotheneuf Harbor: a lengthy detour on the road or a careful crossing if the tide is out. At 8:00 the next morning, there was almost no water in the bay at all, so I doffed my boots and set out, passing stranded sailboats, great heaps of seaweed, and a fellow on a bike.

Then I rounded one rocky headland after another, tramped across secluded beaches, picnicked, and occasionally passed walkers who wished me *bon courage*. On the 130-foot cliffs at the Pointe du Grouin, I spotted a pimple on the broad flat bay to the northeast and realized ecstatically that it was Mont St. Michel.

That day was the walk's high point, partly because it ended in charming Cancale, overlooking the oyster beds of Mont St. Michel Bay. It has a long pier and waterfront main street lined by dozens of seafood restaurants and hotels, like the pleasant, old fashioned La Houle, where I wearily settled in. Then too, there was the special I ordered at a cafe called Le Herpin, just a few doors away, consisting of six oysters on the half shell, bread, and a glass of Muscadet. When I finished, I asked the waitress to bring me the same thing again, and watched dusk paint the bay exquisitely soft shades of blue.

The oystermen were out when I left early the next morning. But soon a stiff wind kicked up, and the GR34 began to follow the busy coast road, which I found unpleasant. So I was relieved to reach the village of Cherrueix, with the bay at its front door and verdant polderlands at its back. L'Hebergement turned out to be a 200-year old farm with six pretty rooms in a renovated stone barn. The astute proprietress quickly assessed my situation, and by breakfast the next morning had gotten me a ride as far as Pontorson, about five miles east of Mont St. Michel, with two other guests from Paris. This allowed me to reach my destination around noon, and I still got to approach the great abbey on foot, like a pilgrim, among sheep grazing at the sides of the modern causeway that permanently connects it to the mainland.

Building commenced at Mont St. Michel eight years before the Norman Conquest and continued through the Middle Ages, which is why the glorious church, cloister, refectory, and guest hall reflect both the Romanesque and the Gothic styles. I took the tour, stood on the ramparts to check the tide (which can recede as much as 10 miles), and had lunch at La Mere Poulard on the Grande rue beneath the abbey.

The restaurant is famous throughout France for its omelets, and shockingly expensive. But I decided I'd earned it. So I ordered the fixed-price menu that included a plain, incredibly frothy omelet tasting slightly of wood smoke, bread, and a slice of chocolate gateau. Afterwards, sated and happy, I caught the bus back to St. Malo.

The trip took only an hour, passing many places I'd walked by. But if I'd traveled by bus both ways, I wouldn't know that there is purple clover at the Pointe de la Varde and lovely soft muck at the bottom of Rotheneuf Harbor.

LOST CANYONS

From Glen Canyon Bridge on US Highway 89, you can see both sides of an argument. To the north is placid Lake Powell, a big, blue tropical cocktail in the arid no-man's-land of southeastern Utah. It's Exhibit A in the case for letting Glen Canyon Dam stand. To the south is the Colorado River, testily emerging from impoundment, cutting through sheer rock walls on its way to the Grand Canyon—wild and free, the way nature made it.

I stood there with my brother, John, one morning in early February, thinking about Seldom Seen Smith, the fictional mastermind of a plot to blow up the Glen Canyon Dam in Edward Abbey's 1975 novel, *The Monkey Wrench Gang.*

Abbey wrote that Smith, "remembered the golden river flowing to the sea, . . . canyons called Hidden Passage and Salvation and Last Chance, . . . strange great amphitheaters called Music Temple and Cathedral in the Desert. All these things now lay beneath the dead water of the reservoir, slowly disappearing under layers of descending silt."

The book has achieved cult status among lovers of Utah's slickrock plateau and canyon country. But Abbey's book never predicted that almost 50 years after the dam's creation, nature, in the form of a blistering six-year drought, would toy with the fate of Lake Powell.

It was 2005. The last time the reservoir had been full—at 3,700 feet above sea level—was in July 1999. In those years, drought had lowered the water level 144 feet, leaving the reservoir at about 33 percent capacity, shrinking the length of the lake from 186 miles to 145 miles and gradually re-exposing something remarkable underneath: the arches and spires of Glen Canyon.

People travel halfway around the world to see the canyon of China's Yangtze River, doomed by construction of the Three Gorges Dam. So was it any wonder that John and I felt compelled to go backpacking in little side canyons on the fringes of Lake Powell, where the water was rapidly receding? It was a chance in a lifetime to see something that couldn't be seen five years before and that may not be seen ever again.

February isn't prime time on Lake Powell, and just getting to the place where we planned to start backpacking required us to take a motorboat 90 miles up the reservoir to its confluence with the Escalante River. Then, among a maze of unmarked tributaries, we had to find Davis Gulch—a stream that enters the Escalante on the west side—take the boat as far into the channel as possible, tie up, and make our way across the quicksand that tends to accumulate at the mouths of such creeks.

There, we were supposed to meet Bill Wolverton, a Glen Canyon National Recreation Area backcountry ranger, who would hike in from the west to show us around for two days. He had responded to a request from John for information about backpacking in Davis Gulch and Fiftymile Canyon, two deeply embedded Escalante River tributaries where a red Navajo sandstone sculpture gallery similar to the one that once lined the whole of Glen Canyon was gradually being re-exposed.

Wolverton had spent the past 17 springs and autumns prowling around the lower 48 states for the National Park Service and could scale sheer canyon walls without working up a sweat. He almost single-handedly launched an effort to eradicate invasive, nonnative plants from the Escalante River canyons he loves. Just don't call the big body of water at his doorstep "Lake Powell." "It's not a lake," he insists. "Lakes are natural features."

Before I could formulate reservations—How cold would it be in southeastern Utah in February? What if it snowed?

How far would we have to hike and how many nights would we camp?—Wolverton and John had started planning the trip.

After taking in the view from the bridge, John and I stopped at the nearby recreation area's Carl Hayden Visitor Center. To enter, we had to pass through a security system tighter than any I've seen at airports, instituted some years ago to deter terrorist attacks on the dam. We apprehensively noted the posted weather forecast—temperatures between 35 and 49 degrees, with rain or snow in the offing. We studied a 1990 topographical model of Lake Powell, hopelessly anachronistic because of shrinking water levels, and took a short tour of the 710-foot-high dam, completed in 1963.

It was led by a sandy-haired young man who told us the concrete of Glen Canyon Dam was good for two millenniums but sediment buildup could render the dam inoperable in 700 years.

Environmentalists are less conservative. They say silt coming in from the reservoir's tributaries could clog it up in a few centuries, never mind that the dam has already damaged habitats and geology at the Grand Canyon, one hundred miles downstream.

Partly for this reason, even environmentalists with cooler heads than Seldom Seen Smith have advocated decommissioning the dam and draining the reservoir—a drastic measure that, nevertheless, has been carried out in the last few decades at about 100 dams across America.

For the thirsty dwellers of the dry Southwest, the specter of losing a water and energy source may be upsetting. The dam's power plant produces $90 million worth of electricity a year, and Lake Powell serves as a holding tank for Lake Mead downriver, a big water supplier to Southern California. Beyond that, the reservoir has undeniable recreational value. But since the onset of the drought, visitation to million-acre Glen Canyon National Recreation Area had decreased from 2.6 million in 1999 to 1.8 million in 2004.

Meanwhile, the National Park Service, which manages the recreation area, was making the best of things by extolling the wonders of newly reclaimed sights while busily extending boat launch ramps at northerly marinas, such as Bullfrog. "Visitors can still enjoy and participate in the same activities that they did when the lake was full—boating, fishing, hiking, camping, and exploring," Kitty L. Roberts, recreation area superintendent, told me.

But it all depended on the weather.

That February, the water level stood at 3,561 feet, just 71 feet above the lowest point at which the dam can generate electricity. "If it drops below that, we're out of business until the lake comes back up," said Tom Ryan, a hydrologist for the US Bureau of Reclamation, which built and operates the dam.

Despite heavy winter snowfall in southwest Utah, Ryan said, it looked like an average year for runoff, which routinely plumps the level of Lake Powell in July. He expected the reservoir to rise about 40 to 45 feet by then, though at that rate it still would take years for the lake to refill.

"And if we have a hot, dry spring, that estimate will be eroded. There's still a lot of uncertainty," he said.

From the dam, John and I drove five miles north to Wahweap Marina, the winter nesting place of huge, luxurious houseboats, some with DVD playerss, staterooms, and fireplaces. There we claimed the far more modest 18-foot powerboat I had reserved for our trip up the reservoir.

Opponents of the man-made reservoir call it "Lake Latrine" and "Lake Foul," but I can't agree with their aesthetic evaluation. It's majestic, with tucked-away coves and beaches backed by surrealistically shaped mesas and buttes. On the way, though, we saw Lake Powell's bathtub ring, a white calcium carbonate deposit left by the receding water, distinct in some places, already wearing away in others.

At Dangling Rope Marina, we stopped for a $100 fill-up. The attendant, who hadn't seen any visitors in days, told us about a good place to camp in Oak Canyon, a few miles farther, on the east side of the lake.

While tying up the boat there, I got caught in some Lake Powell quicksand, which has the consistency of cellulite and is sticky enough to suck in a short person, like me, to the thighs.

John and I pitched our tents, cooked up one of those

wretched, dehydrated backpacker dinners, and went to bed. Unfortunately, it snowed that night and my tent leaked, leaving me with stiff joints, a sour mood, and a wet sleeping bag. I was ready to abort the trip in the morning, but John thought we should at least try to make our scheduled rendezvous with Wolverton at noon in Davis Gulch.

So I went on to Lake Powell's confluence with the Escalante. Along the way, we passed Hole-in-the-Rock Arch, where Mormon pioneers cut a treacherously steep wagon trail from the plateau above to the river in 1880, and the mouth of the San Juan River on the east side—both places I'd only imagined in my dreams. We went astray a few times, but finally found the Escalante and turned in. Between periods of drizzle, the sun came out, revealing bright blue skies and scudding clouds. But the rivers' meeting at Davis Gulch was an ugly scene, choked with flood-strangled cottonwood trees.

Then I saw what I assumed to be a hallucination: a man in a blue shirt, picking his way across the quicksand.

It was Wolverton, a canyon rat if ever there was one, strong and scrawny, with a thatch of shaggy brown hair. He had kindled a campfire up the gulch, where I warmed my feet and hands, dried out my sleeping bag, and decided that, having come this far, it would be folly not to continue.

Wolverton, the only backcountry ranger in the Escalante River region of Glen Canyon National Recreation Area, had been keeping a close watch on sinking water levels in area tributaries. But the last time he climbed down into Davis Gulch and Fiftymile Canyon was the previous summer. Like us, he was eager to see what new glories the drought had revealed.

La Gorce Arch came first, a triangular window on the sky framed in lustrous sandstone, 100 feet wide and 75 feet high. Just a few years ago, when Davis Gulch was fuller, it could be reached only by kayak. Now, as nature intended, you have to crane your neck to see it from the creek bed.

Hiking up the gulch was sloppy, so we exchanged our boots for rubber sandals and neoprene socks. Sometimes the walls of the canyon narrowed, forcing us to wade in the cold water. Then they'd open back up, flooding the chasm with warming sunlight from the plateau hundreds of feet above.

"This place is like a big Christmas present gradually being unwrapped," said Wolverton, stopping short once and opening his arms wide.

On formerly inundated rock ledges, spring-green vegetation had taken root and the bathtub ring had faded. Underfoot, we crunched "canyon popcorn," perfectly proportioned balls of pebbles, a little like candied apples, fused together with mud on their roiling way downstream.

Farther up the gulch, we saw mounds of silt the size of tanker trucks, trapped and then left behind by the retreating water of Lake Powell, which has more silt-bearing tributaries than Lake Mead, another reservoir on the Colorado River impounded by Hoover Dam.

"Sediment is the reservoir's fate," Wolverton said. "It doesn't matter how much boaters want [the lake] or how much water people need. It's going to silt up and the whole thing will be gone."

Wolverton led us out of Davis Gulch on a steep, old slick-rock stock trail. The world seemed different—more horizontal—when we reached the top of the plateau. I could see places I'd known before only on a map: the long rise of Waterpocket Fold to the north and the tiered flanks of the Kaiparowits Plateau to the south, looking in the snow like a Mexican girl's petticoat.

It was flat and easy going for about two miles north across the plateau, but then we came to the edge of Fiftymile Canyon and started down. No old stock trail there, just sure-footed Wolverton to follow.

He had already chosen our campsite for the next two nights, a wide, narrow shelf high above the stream, sheltered by a lip of rock. Delicious, cold, drinkable water was available from a seep in a nearby cliff, and there were plenty of secluded spots on the bank for a camping-style sponge bath. Fire rings and graffiti—including a well-rendered Donald Duck—testified that others had been there before us. Mostly boaters, Wolverton said.

So we settled into a place that even the most widely traveled soul could never forget. Protected by the overhang, we did without tents, though in my down bag I slept in three layers of shirts, two pairs of pants, gloves, and a hood. When I occasionally woke in the middle of the night, I saw a star-spangled crescent of black sky at my bedside.

We spent the next day exploring Fiftymile Canyon, which is even more beautiful than Davis Gulch—much narrower in places, like the Subway, a stretch where three people can't walk abreast. The stream undercuts both sides of the creek there, and the canyon is wider at the base than at the top, limiting the light that filters in and bounces eerily between the walls.

Occasionally, I thought with dread about the prospect of climbing out of Fiftymile, recrossing the plateau, descending into Davis Gulch by the stock trail, and then retrieving the boat for the trip back down the reservoir. But there was the carrot of a steak dinner and clean sheets at a motel in nearby Page. More compelling was the here and now in one of the loveliest places on Earth.

I've seen the Sahara Desert and Denali in Alaska. But none of that tops Fiftymile.

I can't wholly agree with houseboaters who think Lake Powell is paradise or with canyon rats like Wolverton who would be glad to see it shrivel up like a strip of fried bacon.

For now, Mother Nature seems to have decided against the reservoir. I take great consolation in knowing there's no gainsaying her.

❖ 3 ❖

SUNRISE AT BOROBUDUR

Four a.m. is a terrible time of day, too late for night owls, too early for early birds. The exception is 4 a.m. at Borobudur, waiting for the sun to rise with 504 figures of Buddha over the Kedu Plain in central Java.

The temple is one of Southeast Asia's three great religious sites, but older and more esoteric than Bagan in Myanmar and Cambodia's Angkor Wat. Construction began in the eighth-century AD by the Saliendras, a dynasty of Buddhist kings who ruled central Java for almost 200 years until their power waned and the temple was abandoned.

The massive, stepped pyramid rises in nine levels to a single bell-shaped stupa, or tower, surrounded by galleries around which pilgrims walk, meditating on stone reliefs that tell the life story of Siddhartha Guatama, an Indian prince who transcended life's pain to become the Lord Buddha.

You can circle the monument with them or climb to the top, but only by looking at a diagram can you tell that the temple is shaped like a mandala, a mystical scheme of the Buddhist cosmos, with three levels demarking states of consciousness from suffering to enlightenment. Little is known beyond that, leaving the cosmos locked while the temple silently reigns over the volcano-ringed garden of Java.

I told friends I was going to Southeast Asia to see Angkor, a mission accomplished. But for no reason I understood, my real objective was Borobudur, less well-known and off the beaten track, in the world's most populous Islamic country, a feared breeding ground for Al Qaeda. Not only that, Indonesia is one of the most natural disaster-prone places on earth, from Krakatoa west of Java to the 9.0 earthquake off the coast of Sumatra that launched the 2004 tsunami, killing 230,000 people in 14 countries across Southeast Asia. A few days after my visit to Java, there was a major eruption of Mt. Merapi, over whose shoulder I saw the sun rise from the top of Borobudur.

Given all that, it was a surprisingly dreamy trip, organized by Borobudur Tour and Travel, a company I found online with a pleasingly laid-back approach. They offered a three-day itinerary in central Java, including a van, a driver, and hotels, for $375, no deposit required.

The rainy season had just begun when I flew from Singapore to Yogyakarta, about 35 miles southeast of Borobudur. In the arrival hall at the airport, I spotted a man holding a sign that said *Spano*. He turned out to be my amiable driver and guide Noor.

From the airport, we took the traffic-clogged, two-lane ringed road around Yogyakarta, passing cottage industries making wood furniture and temple statue replicas; a boy riding a small merry-go-round mounted on the back of a bike; greengrocery huts with exotic produce piled high; and deeply engorged rivers where children bathed and women in colorful headscarves did the wash. Rice paddies were filled with water to the brim and set like cloudy cut opals in blazing green fields.

For a warm-up, we stopped at Prambanan, a temple complex close to Yogyakarta built shortly after Borobudur, but architecturally more like Angkor Wat, with five artichoke-shaped stupas. The earthquake-damaged compound, partly covered by shaky bamboo scaffolding, looked as if it could collapse in the next tremor.

Noor said *"hati hati,"* which means "be careful" in Indonesian, then waited while I climbed the central stupa and paid my respects to a ten-foot tall statue of the Hindu god Shiva with four hands and a third eye in the center of his forehead. Together with Buddhist Borobudur, this chiefly Hindu place of worship testifies that theological mélange was in the air on Java during the Middle Ages, with the two faiths bleeding into each other until Islam took root around 1400.

The Yogyakarta region, with a population of about 3 million, is the only Indonesian province still ruled by a sultan, a special status recognizing the role the region played in the war for independence against the Dutch. The city is now home to several universities, which give it a smart, young air. But its center remains Sultan Hamengkubuwana's palace (or *kraton*), a walled, white-washed compound of open-air pavilions with its own bank, military garrison, museum of mostly hideous gifts given to sultans, 20 vehicles in the royal garage, and 75 birdcages.

On a tour arranged by Noor, an official palace guide pointed out the décor's myriad male and female symbols and told me that the present sultan has just one wife and five daughters, unlike his father, another Hamengkubuwana, who had 21 children with four concubines.

Afterward, I caught a bicycle cab (or *becek*), the most common, cheap, and practical form of transportation in teeming Yogyakarta, down the long, distracting hurly-burly of Malioboro Road. Lined by tightly packed rows of buildings with Dutch stepped gables, New Orleans-style balconies, galleries full of food, and souvenir vendors—all cheerfully suffering the effects of recent earthquakes and tropical desuetude—this main street quickly became one of my favorite places to shop in the world. I bought light cotton shirts and trousers for about $5 at the Matahari department store, a bouquet of camellias from a flower stall, cheap batik scarves on display on the pavement, and a basket in the dark local market.

I stayed for two nights at a hotel with a sign that said it had hot water on Sosrowijayan Street just off Malioboro, an enclave for scruffy-looking backpackers. Pedestrian alleyways off Sosrowijayan are full of countertop tour agencies, cheap guest houses, and cafes selling second-hand copies of Erich Segal's *Love Story*, Rick Steves' 1986 guide to Europe, Western-style breakfasts, and uniformly terrible coffee. Unwilling to accept that you can't get a good cup of Joe on the island of Java, I roamed widely around the soulful, animated city, never finding it but filling my new basket with additional treasures.

Finally, it was time for the main event: Borobudur, a few hours by van from Yogyakarta. In rice paddies, corn fields, and coconut plantations, near a ramshackle village strung along a bumpy road, it is one of the least touristy UNESCO World Heritage Sites I've visited. I didn't see a single hotel until we entered the temple gate and parked at a cluster of low buildings set around beds of orange cannas. This turned out to be the Manohara guest house, originally built for researchers and architectural historians, who completed a major renovation of the temple in 1983 meant to keep it standing for another 1,000 years. Now open to travelers, the guest house provides a welcome drink of Coca-Cola with tamarind, modest rooms, good food in an open-air dining room, a video introduction to Borobudur, and easy access to the temple, especially for people who want to see it at sunrise.

We arrived in the late afternoon, under heavy black clouds threatening a downpour. Nevertheless, I headed straight for the temple, hidden by trees until the very threshold. Then Borobudur made its appearance, a great layer cake of mottled grey stone supporting a mountain of needle-pinnacled *stupas*.

The arched staircases from level to level are treacherously steep, overlooked by gaping-mouthed gargoyle water spouts, nymphs (or *apsaras*), dancing arms akimbo, and niches enshrining Buddha figures, each with hands in different symbolic poses (or mudras). His life story unfolds on the middle level, starting at the left side of the east entrance, with stone panels of great vividness, recalling the medieval Bayeux tapestry in France. I ran my hand over a carving of Queen Maya in a carriage headed for Lumbini Park, where she gave birth to the Buddha.

Just then a bolt of thunder thwacked, à la *Macbeth,* and guards began herding visitors to a gate far from the one I'd entered. When I told one of them that I needed to get back to the Manohara, he offered to take me there on his motor scooter, the ride of a lifetime circumnavigating the temple.

That night, I watched the Borobudur video; had a *satay* dinner at the restaurant, accompanied by gamelan music, and claimed a flashlight at the front desk for my sunrise visit to Borobudur. I slept soundly, without the interruptions I normally experience on the eve of a great event.

Dawn was still an hour away when I joined a small group of guests in the lobby and followed a guide across the lawn to the temple. He made no comment; there was nothing to say—except, perhaps, "*hati hati.*"

This time, I climbed to the top levels, which are round, not rectangular, and bare except for their forest of stupas, perforated to allow peeks at Buddha statues inside.

Experts say that Borobudur's more abstract upper precincts, especially its empty central stupa, reflect nirvana, a state of being beyond human consciousness. But how could they know? How could anyone know, even sitting atop the temple watching the sunrise pool in a pink halo around soon-to-erupt Mt. Merapi, leaving the mystery of the cosmos secure.

If there is a keyhole anywhere, I'd wager it's at Borobudur.

ACROSS THE TOP OF LOS ANGELES

There is no one way to understand Los Angeles, no one way to take it all in, no one iconic view. Congested highways link its disparate parts without providing a sense of what lies in between. On their shoulders, a fellow in an overheated Mercedes summons a tow truck on his iPhone and a homeless woman brandishes a sign that says, *Stranded, flat broke, need help*.

But for those who seek a road to clarification, there is Mulholland Highway, ribboning across the east-west–tending mountain range that separates the L.A. basin from the San Fernando Valley. Rising to about 3,000 feet, the Santa Monicas are not high, but they are strategically placed, beginning near Dodger Stadium and ending at the Pacific Ocean in Malibu.

Driving its sinuous 55-mile course is the enterprise of one very busy day. Parks and scenic overlooks line the way, and the city unrolls on either side of you like an animated map. Close at hand on the eastern end are the "ego homes" of the rich and famous, clawing their way up the steep, chaparral-covered flanks of a swatch of the Santa Monicas called the Hollywood Hills. Farther west, Mulholland tightrope-walks across Sepulveda Pass and the San Diego Freeway, peters out to dirt for nine miles above Encino, then emerges paved again, taking travelers on a wild, wheel-gripping ride through the mostly undeveloped heart of the mountains.

As a scenic parkway, Mulholland abjures commercial development. However, sustenance for the body and fuel tank is available by turning off on any of the arteries that intersect it and lead down to the nonstop blandishments of Ventura Boulevard in the Valley or those siren thoroughfares to the south, Sunset and Hollywood.

An excursion along Mulholland is best started early, before the Hollywood Freeway clogs. The Mulholland exit lies about 10 miles northwest of downtown L.A., in the narrows of Cahuenga Pass, near where Cecil B. De Mille scouted locations for the 1913 picture, *The Squaw Man*, riding a horse and carrying a six-shooter to fend off rattlesnakes. The exit siphons drivers left off the highway; should you err so soon on the trip and turn right, you'll lose Mulholland altogether, and end up in a maze of residential lanes surrounding the Hollywood Reservoir—a fine place for a morning walk or jog, with the letters of that serendipitous monument, the Hollywood sign, poking out between Italian cypresses.

Left onto Mulholland is the correct direction to go. This way, you'll ride the road west, chasing the sun, starting with its rise at the Hollywood Bowl Overlook, about a mile beyond the highway on the shoulder of a somewhat stubby peak, tauntingly called Mt. Olympus. It is hard to imagine a better view of the L.A. basin, unless it's from a picture window lining the living room of one of the cantilevered homes in the neighborhood. Downtown is a smog-bound mushroom struggling up from the ceaseless grid of streets; Hollywood rolls toward your feet like a weird wave; and in a cup-like declivity to your left once known as Daisy Dell, the Bowl nestles. Freeloaders come to this overlook to listen to the L.A. Philharmonic on summer nights. In the amphitheater below, boxes go for $3,000 to $5,000 a season, and are often hotly contested when their married occupants divorce.

Here on Mt. Olympus, you're in a residential section of Hollywood that came of age in the 50s and 60s. Turn down any lane and you'll find a marvelous, ridiculous cacophony of architectural styles that range from ersatz Georgian to Mayan revival. The architect Richard Neutra blamed the movies for the extravagant proliferation of building styles, and he is not alone in speculating that L.A. home builders see their lots as sets. But as Noel Coward said, "There is always something so delightfully real about what is phony here. And something so phony about what it real."

Indeed, the more you house-hunt in the fabulously well-to-do neighborhoods that line Mulholland Drive, the more the ironies explode, particularly when you contemplate Hollywood's humble beginnings as the inspiration of Horace and Daeida Wilcox, from Topeka, Kansas. In 1887, the Wilcoxes purchased 160 acres that would become central Hollywood, envisioning a Christian subdivision, free from alcohol and vice. The holly bushes Daeida planted did not thrive, and the community took unanticipated turns.

A mile beyond the Hollywood Bowl Overlook on the left is the northern entrance to Runyon Canyon Park, with paths that lead down into the thick of Hollywood, passing a Mission Revival-style mansion built by Gurdon Wattles in 1905 and a rag-tag community garden in a strange neighborhood for communism.

Two miles farther, at the Universal City Overlook, travelers are rewarded with a new perspective, this time to the north. Once Errol Flynn, whose ranch lay nearby, might have stood at this windy eerie surveying the San Fernando Valley. But it's a different view now—developed to the very brink of the surrounding mountains, crowded with malls, gas stations, and TV studios, and crisscrossed by boulevards.

Their very names tell a tale that's pure L.A., about a handful of wealthy Angelinos like J. B. Lankershim and I. N. Van Nuys who owned property in the Valley at the close of the 19th century. In a move that would have fatally dehydrated the city, they claimed the right to the water in the Los Angeles River—despite the fact that on most days it looks like one of those California streams Mark Twain said you could fall into and emerge from "all dusty."

The Supreme Court settled the dispute in favor of the city, but as you contemplate the valley, water is never far from mind. The highway you're traveling was the inspiration of William Mulholland, an Irish ditch digger who taught himself enough engineering to serve as superintendent of the L.A. Water

Department from 1886 to 1928. His best known project was the 250-mile long Owens Valley Aqueduct, which turned the dry San Fernando Valley as green as any well-tended suburban lawn. Today, many view its construction as a crime, since underhanded means were used to gain control of Owens River water while a number of leading citizens cut lucrative, if shady, Valley real estate deals. But in 1913, the city lionized Mulholland, even wooed him to run for mayor, with one councilman claiming that, "His name should be engraved on every water faucet in the city of L.A." He got a highway instead. At the opening of Mulholland Drive on December 27, 1924, bands played, airplanes buzzed, and a ballroom dance champion danced the Spanish tango.

Before abandoning the Universal City way station, turn around and look up. Pinioned by one slender column to a near vertical cliff is an octagonal house known as Chemosphere. Designed in 1960 by John Lautner, it looks like a flying saucer frozen in the process of touching down; very striking, but one wouldn't relish bringing the groceries in.

Two miles beyond Chemosphere, Laurel Canyon Boulevard crosses Mulholland, and it's here that one begins to notice the preponderance of wagging tails in the front seats of cars. Most of them are headed a mile west to Laurel Canyon Park, where dogs, not people, are sovereign, allowed to run free before ten and after three. There, one dog owner told me that her Westie, Bam Bam, always comes home from the park with fleas. But the place is a human, as well as a canine, scene where movie producers are said to hit on pretty women and an ice cream truck dispenses Italian ices.

The San Fernando Valley reveals itself again at the Fryman Canyon Overlook, a mile down the road, this time in a direct headshot, with a backdrop of the San Gabriel Mountains, Santa Susanas, and Simi Hills (from right to left). Off to the northwest too far away to see, some 20 miles over the Ventura County line, lies another piece of the Mulholland story, this one tragic—the ruins of the St. Francis Dam, which collapsed on March 12, 1928, killing 450 and costing the city of L.A. $5 million in damage reparations. This was the last of "the Chief's"

19 dams, and ironically, he visited it on the very day it gave way, pronouncing it sound. Afterward, he took full responsibility for the catastrophe, retiring from the water department, a broken man. The 1974 movie *Chinatown*, in which a character based on "the Chief" is murdered by nefarious water diverters, commenced the refurbishment of Mulholland's reputation. More recently, J. David Rogers, a geological engineer who spent 15 years studying the St. Francis Dam site, reported that a landslide no one could have predicted was the true cause of the disaster.

The highway narrows perceptibly between Fryman Canyon Overlook and Coldwater Canyon Drive so that it seems you're tightrope walking along the very backbone of the mountains, rubbernecking toward the valley at one hairpin turn, and L.A. at the next. Up here, where the rich lust to live, home building continues apace—real estate crunch and all—much to the dismay of the conservationists who are trying to preserve the scenic integrity of the road. Bulldozers eat away whole hillsides in a procedure known as mountain cropping, which provides level space for foundations. Still, there is green up ahead at Coldwater Canyon and Franklin Canyon Parks, which together provide a walking route all the way over the mountains from the Valley to Beverly Hills.

Coldwater Canyon is the enclave of a group of nature-loving volunteers called TreePeople, dedicated to making the world more arborous. I sat in on a session during which an instructor explained planting techniques to a group of school-children, each clutching his or her own sapling. "Don't put them under a telephone pole," she told them, "or next to your swimming pool."

Minutes down the road is the entrance to Franklin Canyon Park, surrounding what was a reservoir, until the earthquake of 1971 convinced the Department of Water and Power that it didn't want to be blamed if a dam busted above Beverly Hills. Now the upper section is the domain of the William O. Douglas Outdoor Classroom, which offers nature appreciation classes for kids and stress relief walks for adults. You can drive all the way down Franklin Canyon, passing through a section of greenbelt where Claudette Colbert and Clark Gable tested their hitchhiking skills in *It Happened One Night*. At the time, the area was owned by oilman Edward L. Doheny, who used to ride up the canyon on horseback from Greystone, his mock Tudor palace below.

Actually, it makes sense to come down off Mulholland at this point for a little replenishment. Coldwater and Franklin Canyon Drives, and Beverly Glen Boulevard a bit farther on, dump you out of the mountains within striking distance of the Beverly Hills Hotel and the equally ritzy, if somewhat more retiring, Hotel Bel Air. But those with a macabre bent should take Benedict Canyon Drive, winding past hedge-shrouded homes that do not want to make your acquaintance; signs on the fences outside proclaim the virtues of their security systems and guard dogs. A little more than halfway down on the right is Cielo Drive, where one August morning in 1969, a cleaning woman discovered the grisly remains of the Manson family killing spree at #10050.

If you still have an appetite after that, and prefer picnics to power lunches, stop for provisions at the little shopping center just south of where Mulholland crosses Beverly Glen. There's another overlook on Mulholland a mile west of this intersection with a bench placed high up like a throne, where you can break into lunch, contemplate Stone Canyon Reservoir, and possibly catch your first sight of the Pacific.

You have now covered only a third of Mulholland—the dense, civilized section. But just as the Santa Monicas widen and rise and you prepare to step on the gas, the pavement stops at Encino Hills Drive about a mile beyond the San Diego Freeway. Happily, even without four-wheel drive, you can rumble on across dirt Mulholland, because it's navigable, except in foul weather. And you should, because here the mountains begin to reveal their wild side, as well as their controversial nature. For years, community groups and the Santa Monica Mountains conservancy have worked to head off development at every pass with the ultimate goal of creating a national park.

One of the parcels of land the Conservancy bought lies about a mile past the end of the concrete, on San Vicente Mountain.

There, perched high above Mandeville, Rustic, and Sullivan Canyons, is an old lookout station for the Nike Missile System, boldly commanding a view of the Pacific. The lookout hasn't been restored and is off limits, but even from its stanchions, the sights are terrific in all directions, including backwards along the winding course of Mulholland. From this point, mountain bikers and walkers take off on a network of paths and fire roads that lead down into Topanga Canyon Park. On the other side of the road is the bright blue surface of Encino Reservoir, looking very much like the one in which the water-logged body of the fictional William Mulholland was found in *Chinatown*.

Dirt Mulholland rambles on, passing a number of dusty new subdivisions, to emerge in concrete near Topanga Canyon Road. There, you must watch the signs closely to make sure that you stay on Mulholland Highway, as opposed to Mulholland Drive, which strikes off toward the Ventura Freeway. It's about 10 miles to 6,000-acre Malibu Creek State Park. It runs all the way down to the Pacific, with a network of trails that take hikers to Castro Crest, manmade Century Lake, and through a meadow that was once part of a ranch owned by Ronald Reagan. Pink and white mountain lilacs and peregrine falcons were out when I passed that way. Hunter House, the park's information center, is the source for trail maps, but serious hikers will have to return to the Santa Monicas another day, for Mulholland awaits.

In many ways, the eight miles between Las Virgenes and Kanan Dume Roads is the most scenic stretch of Mulholland, and over the years moviemakers have agreed, coming to this vicinity to film movies from *Ruggles of Red Gap* to *Mr. Blanding's Dream House*. What is so remarkable about this countryside is its versatility—parts of it look like Australia's Outback, parts like Tuscany and the English moors. Three miles past Las Virgenes is Cornell Road, the turnoff for the Paramount Ranch, now a park complete with a western town set where Borax's *Death Valley Days* was shot. Just beyond Cornell, Sugarloaf Mountain rises. To the left is the entrance for a diminutive private enclave called Malibu Lake, developed as a weekend retreat for movie folk by Cecil B. De Mille. The lake and cabins that surround it are surprisingly humble, but one can imagine the mogul leaning against the clubhouse gate in his jodhpurs.

Between Cornell and Kanan Dume Roads, a large tribe of motorcyclists rule Mulholland—as many slumming lawyers as Hell's Angels. Their favorite watering hole is the Rock Store and Vern's Deli, where you can sip a soda as you observe their rituals.

If by now the sun is setting, you'd be well advised to turn left down Kanan Dume Road to the safer, saner pleasures of the coast. On the other hand, there are still 15 death-defying miles of Mulholland to go before Arroyo Sequit Canyon funnels you out on the beach at Leo Carrillo State Park like a piece of mountain jetsam. Honk before rounding all hairpin turns. Watch for the random dumped corpse and rock slides that routinely narrow this stretch of Mulholland to one lane. Ignore the smashing views of the Pacific and the weird satellite dishes that stick out of the canyon like Mickey Mouse ears.

You may be somewhat wired when you reach the Pacific Coast Highway. By now, it might be Magic Hour, that crepuscular time the movies love. Up on Mulholland, the mountain lions and backseat smoochers are coming out, and the lights in the valley and basin are beginning to bloom. You could go back to see night-side Mulholland. After all, the road runs right to L.A., not straight, but true.

❖ 5 ❖

THESE VAGABOND SHOES

Somewhere around the 22,834-foot Aconcagua Peak, I decided that my highway map of Argentina hadn't been a good buy; it was huge and unwieldy, with a tendency to antagonize bystanders when I unfolded it. Also, it showed the whole country—2,300 miles long from the Paraguayan border to Tierra del Fuego in the south—when I needed only a three-inch strip in the middle.

My 1,000-mile route began in Santiago, Chile, and took me over the Andes and across Argentina to Buenos Aires. I left Santiago on a Saturday morning in late February, with little more than a backpack and a bag, that map, and the certainty, gleaned from guidebooks, that it's possible to go almost anywhere in Argentina by bus. Driving the whole way didn't appeal to me. I could have flown, but I wanted to spot a gaucho on the pampas. And although a train does cross from Buenos Aires to Mendoza on the eastern flank of the Andes, there you're stuck (though the disused tracks wind up the wild, lonely canyon of the Mendoza River and over the mountains at the 12,6000-foot Uspallata Pass).

However, Argentine bus companies ply routes that make a spider web of the map, with poetic names like *El Porvenir* (the future), *1 de Mayo* (the first of May), and *La Veloz del Norte* (the speed of the north). So, of course, I romanticized the trip, poring over Bruce Chatwin's *In Patagonia* and studying photographs in travel magazines of Argentine estancias now open as inns. I even got the buses themselves wrong, imagining chickens and bald tires; cheap, Argentine bus travel has more to do with loud, piped-in pop music, mini-skirted stewardesses, and subtitled movies made for American TV. If you pay slightly more, you can book a sleeper bus on overnight journeys, and bus stations in larger towns are remarkable minimalls.

Still, the reality of the trip didn't make it any less an adventure. Were I to do it again, I would give myself more time so that I could detour at will to out-of-the way spots only touched on in guidebooks—birthplaces of famous Argentine statesmen, offbeat religious shrines, and the like. As it was, I saw the Andes, Mendoza, some of the country's best-preserved colonial architecture in Cordoba, and a good deal of countryside.

I came to enjoy rolling into a town, getting a sightseeing map at the tourist information office (situated in most bus stations), and then striking off on foot in search of a hotel room. I was able to see a lot that way and felt free to do precisely as I pleased—although sometimes I made mistakes.

It might have been a mistake to book a more expensive shared taxi from Santiago to Mendoza instead of taking the less expensive bus ride, but a gregarious man in the Santiago bus station convinced me it would trim two hours off the seven-hour trip. I will never forget that ride in a battered chocolate brown Ford Falcon with three other utterly silent passengers and a driver who chain-smoked while I inhaled gas. He drove the Pan American Highway like a maniac, ascending the bone-dry, scrub-covered Andes, where little grows above 11,500 feet, flying around an amazing series of switchbacks leading to the border, and then finessing us through Customs and Immigration by exchanging a few chummy words with a uniformed guard at the barricade. Stunned by the swiftness of the ride and yearning to see the sights, I kept asking, "*Donde esta el Aconcagua? Donde esta el Cristo Redentor?*" Blithely, the driver gestured with his cigarette toward the highest mountain in the Western Hemisphere, but we never saw the statue of Christ erected in the mountains to celebrate the settlement of an Argentine-Chilean border dispute in 1902; it is off the road.

Clearly, if I wanted to see anything along this popular pass through the Andean cordillera, I'd have to go back. This proved easy enough, because Mendoza, where the taxi let me off, is western Argentina's excursion central; from there, scores of tour companies take travelers into the mountains, for visits to the vineyards south of town, on whitewater rafting trips down the Mendoza River, and trekking along the 23-mile northwest approach to Aconcagua.

With limited time, I chose a daylong van tour that retraced the taxi's route northwest along the Mendoza River, this time going slowly enough for me to appreciate the glitteringly metallic mountains. (Suddenly, I understood why Spanish conquistadores felt sure they concealed cities of gold.) We learned about General José de San Marin's Andean guerilla battles with the Spanish in the early nineteenth century at a historic site in the oasis-like hamlet of Uspallata; took a tram ride up the deserted ski slopes at Los Penititentes, with snaggle-toothed peaks on every side; dipped our toes in the yellowish thermal waters at a natural bridge; walked a half-mile up Aconcagua, panting in the thin air; and visited Cristo Redentor. With outstretched arms, the statue gives a benediction to what is surely one of the bleakest places on earth, an abandoned border crossing—though "falling" might be a better word, since from the statue, it's a 13,000-foot drop to Chile.

Meanwhile, inside the van, the portly driver, Alfredo, argued in Spanish about *futbol* and politics with a radio sportscaster from Buenos Aires; when I concentrated, I could almost understand. The newscaster occasionally deigned to talk to me, specifying that he had been taught "English English" in school. On the road back from Cristo Redentor, his girlfriend, a nurse with a shy teenage daughter, took out a vacuum flask of hot water and prepared *mate*, Argentina's tea-like national beverage brewed from the leaves of the *Ilex paraguayensis* plant and drunk through a straw; graciously, she passed me her handy traveling gourd, and I found that I liked the bitter elixir.

I also liked Mendoza, the capital of Mendoza Province, where I spent the day before my mountain tour roaming delightful avenues lined with gnarled plane trees, wide irrigation channels, and tile sidewalks meticulously cleaned every morning with kerosene. In the town's old section (partly spared from frequent, disastrous earthquakes, like the one that virtually leveled Mendoza in 1861), I took in the ruins of a Jesuit mission dating from 1638 and a small but well-designed archaeological museum, followed by a mouthwatering steak at a shady alfresco grill.

I could have seen the sights of Mendoza in one day. But I wasn't quite ready to get on another bus, so I spent the next day visiting the highly mechanized Penaflow winery south of town. I also checked out the central market and marveled over the liver, brains, tripe, and a green squash the size of a baseball bat, then frittered away the afternoon in the Plaza España. Of all Mendoza's many parks, this seemed to me the loveliest, with walkways and benches made of tiles bearing pictures of heraldic shields, sailing ships, and Spanish castles.

That night, I boarded the bus for Córdoba, traversing the arid countryside west of the Sierras de Córdoba through the wee hours. If I had wanted to spend 20 hours rather than 11 on a bus, I could have left in the morning and seen more, but I still had the 10-hour trip to Buenos Aires before me and didn't want my limbs to atrophy. On board, a stewardess served us a dinner of boiled mystery meat, potatoes, and jug wine, then screened an American police flick while I sank into my deeply reclining seat. I would have slept were it not for my seatmate, a salesman who peddled tapes to discos across Chile and Argentina, snored loudly, and spoke English—too often and too well. When he saw that I was reading a novel by Isabel Allende, cousin of Chile's deposed socialist president Salvador Allende, he told me to watch out, or people would think I was a communist.

Around dawn the next morning, we crossed the Sierras, blanketed in trees and thick fog, and then descended toward sprawling Córdoba and the pampas beyond. Bleary-eyed, I made a reservation at the tourist office in the bus station for a room in a modern hotel that had a private bath and included breakfast.

I was getting the sniffles by the time I reached the hotel, and in a cold drizzle, Córdoba seemed grim, as well as noisy and congested. Still, I rallied to tour one of the oldest cities in Argentina, founded in 1573 and for decades thereafter far more vigorous than Buenos Aires, although its architecture is by and large modern now. The buildings on Calle Obispo Trejos that house the Universidad Nacional de Córdoba and Colegio Nacional de Monserrat are Spanish colonial gems, as is the Córdoba Cathedral on the Plaza San Martin, with an impressive three-tiered dome and an exterior that looks like a melting lemon ice cream cone. Next door is the city's handsomely restored Cabildo, where I found a fascinating exhibit on the great bullrings of Spain. Best of all, though, was the display of antique *fanals*—glass-encased baby-Jesus figurines surrounded by dried flowers, fruit, paste jewels, and other colorful geegaws—at the Museo Historico Provincial Marques de Sobremonte.

At noon the next day, I took a seat on a Chevalier bus bound for Buenos Aires. This one didn't show movies or serve food, so I carried a large bottle of mineral water and a package of dainty, crustless ham and cheese sandwiches, kicked off my shoes, and watched the pampas roll by. The flat fields of sunflowers and corn, grain elevators, and fly-speck towns looked so much like those on the North American plains that I kept having to remind myself I wasn't in Kansas anymore. Across the aisle from me, a sweet elderly couple sipped *mate*. Then, as we approached the federal capital, the loudspeaker announced our imminent arrival with Frank Sinatra's rendition of "New York, New York"—which made me laugh out loud as I put my vagabond shoes back on.

❖ 6 ❖

A BAD NIGHT'S SLEEP

The Swedish word for people who come to the Icehotel, 120 miles north of the Arctic Circle, to spend the night is *tokig*. It means "crazy."

The room temperature is 23 degrees. The walls, beds, chairs, light fixtures, even the glasses used in the bar, are made of ice. You can't unpack your clothes because they'd freeze, and the thought of getting out of your sleeping bag to go down the hall to the toilet is enough to keep you awake all night.

Those inconveniences aside, every winter, thousands of people come to Swedish Lapland to sleep in a hotel of snow and ice. The number of rooms varies from year to year, as does the décor, because in the spring the building melts into the nearby Torne River, to be reconstructed in the fall as the spirit moves the ice artists.

The Icehotel—something of an international concept, having spawned similar frozen hostelries in Japan, Norway, Canada, and Romania—was the brainchild of Swedish entrepreneur Yngve Bergqvist, who wanted to find a way to attract winter visitors to a frigid and remote but singularly beautiful place. It began as a humble igloo housing a 1989 art exhibit, where a handful of intrepid souls spent the night and woke up raving about the experience.

In 1994, Absolut Vodka of Sweden came here to shoot ads featuring supermodels like Kate Moss and Naomi Campbell posed in scanty haute couture on minimalist ice chairs and staircases. The campaign was so cool and so successful that *Forbes* named Absolut the number one luxury brand in the world, ahead of Tiffany and BMW. People from Tokyo to Berlin started wondering how they would sleep and what they would dream about on slabs of Swedish ice.

On a plane to Stockholm in January, I told the buttoned-up business man next to me that I was headed north of the Arctic Circle. He loosened his tie and said, "You're not going to one of those ice places, are you?"

From Stockholm, I flew more than 800 miles north to Kiruna, an iron mining town beneath Sweden's highest peak, 6,965-foot Kebnekaise. There, a bus waited to take my fellow travelers and me 10 miles east to Jukkasjarvi, set among snow-coated pine forests and lakes. With a population of 700, it has almost as many sled dogs as people. Along with boisterous 30-something Brits, who outnumber all other nationalities and age groups attracted to the Icehotel, there were Japanese, Germans, and Danes, as well as a few honeymooning couples who planned to spend their nuptial night in a suite of ice.

The sun was setting in delicate Easter egg shades of blue and pink when I arrived about 2 p.m. (In the middle of winter the sun rises about 10 a.m., I later discovered.) The temperature was minus 22. Where the snow had been left unplowed, it came up to my knees; the air was so dry that it scoured my lungs with every breath; my feet were cold, my cuticles were cracked, and my hair was a static electric mess.

I checked in at the reception building. Parked at the door were kick sleds that look like chairs mounted on skis, used for moving luggage and sightseeing in the village. There were Absolut Icehotel ads on the walls, blooming amaryllis in the windows, Swedish minimalist egg chairs, and a wood-burning stove around which people in snowsuits clustered. The receptionist told me to go immediately to the adventure center next door to check out winter gear like theirs.

I got stout lace-up boots, ski gloves, a funny fur hat with earflaps, and a snowsuit under which I was advised to wear several additional layers, starting with thermal long johns. So attired, I looked something like a clown made out of balloons.

I squeaked when I walked, but the outfit kept me toasty during my Icehotel stay.

At the adventure center, I booked a three-hour snowmobile expedition for the next day and a 90-minute dogsled ride for the morning after that. In all, I planned to stay at the Icehotel for three nights: first in a heated cabin, then in an ice chamber, and finally in the lodge, which has all the modern comforts, including a thermostat.

No one, it seems, stays in the Icehotel proper for more than a night. It's camping in the cold at five-star prices, much like an extreme sport you have to psych yourself up for. Afterward, you receive a diploma to prove you've done it. I learned all this by taking the tour for people staying in the Icehotel.

This sprawling, single-story, igloo-like edifice had an arched entry and double doors covered in reindeer skins, illuminated by a chilly blue light. Beyond the hotel entrance was the grand hall, supported by round ice columns about a foot in diameter, decorated with a fiber-optically illuminated ice chandelier that shimmered like diamonds in the dimness. Packed snow corridors burrowed off the grand hall, leading to the domed ice bar, heated luggage room, and toilets, and to the ice chambers.

Like Room 316, where I stayed the next night, most rooms were small and plain. Standard doubles had curtained doorways and two-foot-high ice-block platform beds cushioned by thin mattresses and reindeer pelts. The suites were grander, individually decorated by 35 artists, with sitting areas, sculptures, bizarre fiber-optic lighting fixtures, and furniture, all in ice, of course. One had a Japanese theme, another African. The Shakespeare suite surrounded guests with ice-sculpted scenes from *Macbeth*.

After I was settled, I wandered into the unheated art center next to the hotel. There, Swedish graphic designer Mats Indseth, who created the Shakespeare suite, was chiseling away at a bust of the Bard, intended for a full-scale ice replica of London's Globe Theater, where dance, drama, and musical productions were to be staged. Indseth said he finds Torne River ice an exceptionally malleable, beautifully clear medium for sculpture.

The Torne supplies the 8.8 million pounds of ice used in the construction of the hotel, which is also composed of a highly insulating combination of water and snow blasted onto metal frames that are later removed to make the meter-thick walls and ceilings. The result, once smoothed down and decorated by artists, amazes and enchants most visitors, who can tour the facility during the day. The ice bar is open to everyone until the wee hours of the morning. But after 7 p.m., only hotel guests are allowed to wander the halls, dazed, probably, by the prospect of their impending hibernation.

The tour guide told my group the routine: Once you check in for a night, you drag or kicksled your bags to the luggage room, where you're given a locker. For the rest of the day, you're basically homeless, because the ice rooms are too cold and forbidding for anything other than sleep (and even that's questionable). When it's finally time to retire, you strip to your long johns and grab a sleeping bag designed for temperatures as low as minus 13 degrees; you take it to your chamber; settle in, and wait to nod off.

If you're lucky, the next thing you know it's 7:30 a.m. and an Icehotel staff member is at your bedside with a cup of warm lingonberry juice. Most guests follow it with a stint in the sauna.

That's the ideal Icehotel overnight, at least. Actually, I met one young Englishman who told me he enjoyed 10 uninterrupted hours of slumber in an ice chamber, but his girlfriend said he could sleep like a puppy anywhere. A front desk clerk told me she frequently finds Icehotel refugees sprawled on couches in the reception building. Most people who make it through the night arise with the hollow-eyed look of life-sentence prisoners and practice responses such as, "It was an experience. I'm glad I did it," leaving unsaid the obvious, that they'd never do it again.

But, happily, there's more to the Icehotel than a bad night's sleep. If you're lucky enough to be there under the right conditions, there's the aurora borealis, or the northern lights, a phenomenon caused by electrically charged solar particles drawn into the earth's magnetic field. For the brave, there's a sauna that is run by a German nudist on the premises of the Icehotel where you can sit in a hot tub outdoors, then take a numbing dip in a hole cut through the ice of the Torne River.

Above all, there's Arctic Sweden, a vast, low-lying winter wonderland of pine trees and birches, so sparsely populated that thousands of square miles are used for rocket and aircraft testing and research on global warming and the ozone layer.

Together with parts of Norway, Finland, and Russia, the region is home to the vigorous Sami people, gatherers of cloud-berries and herders of reindeer, whose history in the frozen north of Europe dates at least to the first century. About 17,000 Samis live in Sweden, where, as an ethnic minority, they have struggled to retain their language, culture, and land as home-steaders from the south pushed into Lapland and the Samis' nomadic lifestyle has become increasingly untenable.

Recently, however, there has been a revival of interest in the Samis. The ice Globe Theater has presented an abridged version of Shakespeare's *Hamlet* in the Sami language. The village of Jukkasjarvi has a Sami cultural center with displays devoted to the woodcarving, shamanistic religion, and hunting practices of the indigenous people. Several tours offered by the Icehotel's adventure center introduce visitors to the Sami way of life.

On my snowmobiling adventure, I met Kjell Nutti, a full-blooded Sami, who led the tour. Nutti spends his free time hunting, and said he's been able to stay in the land he loves because of the Icehotel.

He took me and two couples on snowmobiles through the forest and over frozen swamps to a Sami campsite by a lake, where he prepared a lunch of smoked reindeer meat and vege-tables, accompanied by piping hot coffee and tea. Afterward, as we stood in the middle of the iced-over lake, rimmed like a fine china teacup with those shades of blue and pink, it became clear why he loves Swedish Lapland.

Later, my dogsled trip introduced me to the canines of the region. It was led by a young Norwegian, who hitched 12 surprisingly small, spry dogs, all part husky, in front of a wooden sleigh that carried five people sitting astride in a row, including the driver. The dogs howled in disharmonious concert, straining at their halters to get going, and occasionally lapped up snow as they pulled the sleigh over the frozen Torne

River. My favorite was Puss, a black female. I'd never seen a dog with such ghostly pale blue eyes.

Flying past the village, I found it hard to imagine what Jukkasjarvi would look like in the green of summer. Later, when I walked there, bundled up and chugging along like a little engine, I thought that winter actually becomes the place. With smoke rising from chimneys and windowpanes frosted over, the small frame houses seemed quintessentially cozy. In the yard of one home, kids had built an ice palace of their own. And at the far end of town, the 18th-century wooden church, surrounded by a graveyard and a picket fence, slumbered blissfully in a cloak of snow.

Blissful sleep was much on my mind the day of my stay in the ice room. To kill time before turning in, I had a long dinner in the restaurant, handsomely decorated with Swedish antique cabinets, paintings, and sconces. The meal started with smoked salmon stuffed with cream cheese and the house white wine, from Alsace, France. The entrée—grilled tenderloin of beef in Madeira sauce with a terrine of root vegetables—was followed by a dessert of chocolate mousse. Everything about the meal was exceptional, including the service. When I told the waiter I was sleeping in the Icehotel that night, he advised me to pass on after-dinner coffee.

Then there was nothing to do but seek warmth and courage at the ice bar. It had ice tables that look like giant thumbtacks, a reindeer skin-covered banquette, and a beautiful, long curved ice bar with colored liqueurs gleaming from icy shelves. The drinks were elaborate vodka concoctions served in glasses made of beveled-out ice blocks. (A few nonalcoholic beverages were available as well, which have to be stored in the fridge to keep them from freezing.) As elegantly seductive as it looked, there was a decided frisson of fear that could be felt among those headed to ice beds.

I was scared when I downed the last drops of my bear's eye, made of Absolut Citron and blueberry liqueur, and got my sleeping bag; I kept telling myself that no one had died in the Icehotel yet.

In Room 316, I spread out the bag, stuffed an extra sweater

and socks inside, and got in. I zipped up and pulled the string on the hood until only my nose was exposed to the cold air. It was comfy, in a way. So far, so good.

But there was a crease in the back of my long johns I couldn't straighten; the Velcro at the top of the bag kept scratching my lips; I couldn't easily move my feet; and when I tried to turn on my side, I got tangled in the cotton sleep sack lining the bag. I must have dozed off, because at one point I awoke, worried about losing the hole in the hood and being smothered, which kept me from going back to sleep. And then morning came, with the warm lingonberry juice and a diploma.

When I think of the Icehotel, a song from the musical *Gypsy* comes to mind: "You Gotta Have a Gimmick." To get people to lovely Swedish Lapland, you need a gimmick, I guess. I'm thrilled to have been there and glad to have made it through my night. But I'll leave the obvious unsaid.

THE WHITE HORSES OF WILTSHIRE

"There's an old White Horse cut in one side of the highest hill hereabouts and many folks sets a good deal of store by it." The words are those of Thomas Hughes, the 19th-century British writer who gave us *Tom Brown's Schooldays*. Hughes grew up in the village of Uffington, beneath a northern escarpment of the Berkshire Downs, some 50 miles west of London. There, engraved in the earth near the crest of an 859-foot-high prominence known as White Horse Hill, overlooking the undulating Vale of the White Horse, lies one of England's most magnificent and beloved historic monuments: the figure of a horse, abstract but unmistakably equine, careening across the downs.

The creature, which measures 365 feet from ear to tail, is thought to be the work of some ingenious artist, perhaps prehistoric, who scraped away the springy grass on the hillside to reveal the chalky soil underneath. The result is astonishing, for the horse stands out brilliantly white against the lush green turf—kept neatly cropped by accommodating herds of sheep— and is visible on clear days from a distance of 20 miles.

The Uffington Horse, as it's called, inspired other turf artists in more recent times. Taking up shovels and spades, they made their marks on hillsides in Wiltshire, the county to the west of Berkshire, where the downs roll on until they descend toward Salisbury Plain. Eleven large white horses decorate the Wiltshire hills, none so venerable as their sire at Uffington, perhaps, but each with a curious history and character of its own. The white horse at Marlborough, a charming college town tucked into the folds of the downs, is the early 19th-century product of an ambitious group of boy scholars from Mr. Greasley's Academy. At Devizes, a market hub for the agriculturally rich downlands, a horse was cut in 1845 by cobblers' apprentices known as snobs. Now mostly obliterated, it is still referred to as "the Snob's Horse." Several miles away, the Alton Barnes animal, with its big affectionate eye, was commissioned by a wealthy farmer in 1812, though its designer, Jack the Painter, absconded with his payment before the figure was completed. (The shiftless fellow was later hanged.)

Glimpsed in murky weather from the window of a car or train, these hill carvings startle and then pass like a dream; in sunshine, they are like odd pieces of graffiti. Regardless of the elements, though, they make splendid destinations in and of themselves. High upon the downs, they occupy not stables but aeries, and from the top of the trails that climb to them are views of a countryside patterned by church spires and copses, pastures, and fields that have been tilled since the Stone Age.

White Horse explorers can make a base for their downland peregrinations in the towns of Marlborough or Devizes, or in the village of Avebury (at the center of White Horse country), which offers classic bed and breakfast–style accommodations in cottages set among concentric circles of Sarsen stones— a prehistoric monument that, according to the 17th-century antiquarian John Aubrey, exceeds Stonehenge "as a cathedral does a parish church."

There are fine White Horse vantage points along Wiltshire's country roads, of course, but to really know a white horse, you must walk right up to it. Fortunately, the paths to any of the better-kept hill carvings are easy to find and well maintained, though not so obviously trammeled that excursions along them don't seem an adventure. Stout-soled shoes are required, as are ordnance survey maps, those admirable inventions that point out the myriad sights to be investigated along the way: Iron Age fortifications, neolithic burial mounds called barrows, battlegrounds of the great Saxon king Alfred and of the rebel Cromwell, and England's oldest road, the Ridgeway, a 50-mile-long path from Aylesbury to Avebury thought to have been walked by Homo sapiens before 10,000 BC—before, some say, England was an island.

To prepare for the Wiltshire animals, though, you should first make a journey—or a pilgrimage—across the Berkshire border to the Uffington White Horse. As you motor north along the A4361 from Avebury, and then east on the B4507 toward Uffington, remember that:

> *Before the gods that made the gods*
> *Had seen their sunrise pass,*
> *The White Horse of the White Horse Vale*
> *Was cut out of the grass.*

So wrote G. K. Chesterton in *The Ballad of the White Horse*, a modern-day play celebrating the heroic exploits of King Alfred. According to Chesterton and local legend, the Uffington White Horse was carved to commemorate the Saxon warrior's victory over the marauding Danes at Ashdown in 871. Others look further back in history to date the beast, associating it with the battle of Badon Hill, where the Roman Britons—led, perhaps, by Arthur Pendragon himself—routed Alfred's Saxon forebears. Contemporary archaeologists have found echoes of the figure's near hieroglyphic stylization in coins that date from the first century BC.

This most ancient and awesome of England's turf horses is best seen from a distance—on the train bound from Reading to Swindon, say, or from Uffington village. It lies below an Iron Age hill fort, Uffington Castle, a series of concentric ditches and mounds surrounding a wide-open space where the wind whips around a visitor's ears and where in centuries past festivals and white horse cleanings (or scourings) were held every seven years. Country folk sang while they weeded the chalk:

> *The owl White Horse wants zettin to rights,*
> *And the Squire hev promised good cheer,*
> *Zo, we'll gee un a scrape to kip un in zhape,*
> *And a'll last for may a year.*

Afterward, they "chased a cheese" down a combe called "the

Manger," quenched their thirst on ale and cider, and had their pockets picked by gypsies.

Today, the Uffington White Horse is maintained by English Heritage and is reached by a sharply ascending access road off the B4507 that passes an old, flat-topped hill where, legend has it, St. George slew the dragon—a fine spot for a picnic. Above the carving runs the Ridgeway path, taking walkers two miles west to Wayland's Smithy, a prehistoric burial mound composed of huge upright boulders, or a mile east to the Blowing Stone, which Alfred is said to have sounded to rally his troops.

A convenient excursion on the return trip from Uffington to the Wiltshire Downs involves turning east off the A4361 at the village of Broad Hinton, just a few miles north of Avebury. Soon a hill figure appears before you on the gentle slope of Hackpen Hill. This is a much more modest horse, 90 feet by 90, reported to be the work of a parish clerk and a publican who cut it in 1838 to commemorate the coronation of Queen Victoria.

The Hackpen Horse is a relatively naturalistic rendering, though critics have called it foxlike, and serious archaeologists dismiss it as a Victorian "folly." There is a parking lot at the top of the hill, where the Ridgeway intersects the road; nearby, a stile leads into a pasture, which the carving shares with a number of friendly, real-life horses.

A second day of white horse exploration begins with a visit to the Westbury Horse, southwest of Devizes along the A360 and the B3098, leading to the village of Bratton. This is the oldest carving in Wiltshire. A boldly executed creature, 182 feet long and 108 feet high, it mimics the work of the famous 18th-century English horse painter George Stubbs. Placed just below the Iron Age hill fort known as Bratton Castle, the animal commands a "most beautiful prospect" (as Richard Gough, the editor of Camden's *Britannia*, put it) toward Bath over the Vale of Pewsey. Now maintained by the Westbury Lions Club, it can be circumnavigated on foot by the hardy, or surveyed from benches at its flanks.

The carving's peaceful setting belies a heated argument over its origins. A steward for the Lord of Abingdon dug the present horse in 1778, but a sketch that predates this cutting by six years shows a very different animal: a saddled, dachshund-like creature with a serpentine, forked tail. Iconographers suggest that this earlier carving might have been fashioned in prehistoric times, making it perhaps as old or older than Uffington's. The local citizenry attributes it to the well-nigh ubiquitous Alfred, who fought the Danes in this neighborhood in 878. Whatever its true origins, there is almost certainly a horse beneath the horse, and the poor steward who meant only to improve the older figure has taken it on the chin, being called, among other things, a "vandal," "wretch," and "unimaginative busybody."

Two years after the steward refurbished the Westbury cutting, an industrious apothecary named Christopher Alsop decided to create a horse of his own on a steep hill outside the village of Cherhill, just off the A4, approximately five miles west of Avebury. According to the account of a local vicar, Dr. Alsop stood on a precipice a mile away from his hillside canvas with a megaphone, shouting orders to workmen on the site—the entire enterprise earning him the sobriquet "the mad doctor."

To reach the Cherhill figure, park along the A4 where signs appear for the white horse and Oldbury Castle, yet another Iron Age fort. Up top, the 140-foot-long horse, a castle, and a tumbledown obelisk constructed in 1845 by Lord Lansdowne in memory of his ancestor Sir William Petty make an impressive trio of sights. I searched for the Cherhill horse one morning in a thick mist, which parted suddenly to show it at my very feet. Later, I returned in the sunshine to watch as a shepherd opened a gate below and waves of sheep surrounded and engulfed the complacent creature.

Three carvings on the hills around Marlborough compose the agenda for another fine day of white horse touring. Mr. Greasley's Academy is long extinct, but the scholars figure just above the town and the River Kennet is an easy walk from the present Marlborough College, with its lovely grounds and chapel. This horse is only 62 feet long—making it, perhaps, more correctly a pony—and in some disarray, like the school boys who throng through the streets of Marlborough between classes, with their shirttails out and ties rumpled.

The white horse near the village of Alton Barnes, five miles west of Marlborough, is thought to be a copy of its fellow at Cherhill. Jack the Painter's steed, 162 feet from muzzle to tail, canters where hang gliders soar between the dramatic inclines of Walker's and Milk hills, a site that is almost as spectacular as the Uffington setting. To visit the horse, take the A345 south from Marlborough, then turn west on the road to Alton Barnes. At the village, turn north on the Lockeridge road, and soon the creature will appear before you on the left. From Avebury, the Alton Barnes carving can be reached on foot by following a southern spur of the Ridgeway and then cutting west along the Wansdyke, a ditch and mound that once ran for 50 miles toward the Bristol Channel and is thought to have been built by Roman Britons as a line of defense against the Saxons invading from the north.

South of Marlborough along the A345 lies the most modern of Wiltshire's white horses, cut by the Pewsey Fire Brigade in 1937 to commemorate the coronation of George VI. Visitors to this horse, which is 65 feet across and 47 feet high, should turn off the A345 about a quarter of a mile south of the town of Pewsey, following the road to Everleigh. The Pewsey Horse's artist and chief engineer was one George Marples, whose son, Morris, remains the authority on white horse carvings and wrote the indispensable *White Horses and Other Hill Figures*.

According to Morris Marples, five other white horse figures exist among the Wiltshire Downs, but, left unattended, they have been consumed by the rapacious turf, which "crawls and creeps," as Chesterton put it. The communities that have kept their horses tidy are justly proud of their efforts, though during world War II, all the figures were covered with grass and branches to keep German pilots from using them as points of reference.

A variety of hill figures—crosses, World War I regimental badges, lions, and giants—exists in other parts of England, but only in Wiltshire have chalk artists devoted themselves so exclusively to horses. The creatures graze contentedly on the Downs there, ready to amaze and delight visitors who seek them out.

❖ 8 ❖

FRENCH HANOI

A tall, beautiful woman in black and a small Asian girl stand at the prow of a barge moving slowly over a wide, jungle-banked river. The woman is Catherine Deneuve, star of the 1992 movie *Indochine,* about the war for independence in French Vietnam. In 1954, when France finally abandoned its Southeast Asian colony after a humiliating defeat at the hands of Vietnamese nationalists, America stepped in to wage a battle against the same enemy that was billed as an effort to stem the spread of communism.

But for a long time before all that, Vietnam was French, bound together in 1887 with Laos and Cambodia in the Indochinese Union. The relationship ultimately brought misery to all, but in another sense, the colonial era bore gorgeous fruit in the mélange of styles exhibited in every sumptuous scene of *Indochine.*

From roughly 1850 to 1950, the subtle, seductive French-Vietnamese amalgamation infused couture, art, literature, and cuisine. Inevitably, the style traveled back to aesthetically sensitive Paris, where it can still be detected at certain shops, restaurants, and museums.

But to really experience the evanescent style—silken fabrics, slow-moving ceiling fans, louvered windows, tamarind trees, lacquer cigarette holders, and muddy espresso—you have to go to Hanoi, now the capital of the Socialist Republic of Vietnam, formerly the administrative center for the French colony of Indochina.

There the French built wide, tree-lined avenues, grand villas in a hybrid style known as "Norman Pagoda," and a scaled-down replica of the Opera Garnier in Paris. They spread the language of Voltaire, Catholicism, and café society; taught the Vietnamese how to make puff pastry; renamed streets for French dignitaries; and sent the dashing Foreign Legion to patrol those streets.

"After a visit to Hanoi, one is curious to learn what the French would have done to Singapore or Hong Kong if they had possessed them," said the Englishman Alfred Cunningham, who toured the city around 1900.

Nowadays, most Americans visit Vietnam to remember the war that ended when the United States pulled out of Southeast Asia in 1973, to meet the marvelous Vietnamese people on friendlier terms, to see pagodas, to trek in the mountains, to shop for curios, and to relax on a South China Sea beach. But while living in Paris, I went to Hanoi to seek out what remains of French Vietnam before it vanishes under the rising tide of modernization.

Vietnam stagnated after Communist consolidation, but 1986 free market reforms made the economy roar. In 2005, the country celebrated 25 successive years of growth, which has had predictable results. Construction and pollution are rampant, especially in Saigon (Ho Chi Minh city) and the south. If the north seems to lag behind, it is only because it got off to a late start.

It is still possible to wander like a *flaneur* through Hanoi's Old Quarter on the north and west sides of Hoan Kiem Lake, watching the Vietnamese cook, eat—indeed, live their lives— on the uneven sidewalks. The habit of alfresco dining presumably made the Vietnamese receptive to French sidewalk cafés; everywhere, people sit at tables under umbrellas that advertise *La Vie* brand bottled water. As in Montmartre and St. Germain des Pres, they chain smoke, dispute, and drink coffee, though here it's the Vietnamese brew, so thick that it looks black even after the barman puts in milk.

I started my search in the Old Quarter at the amiable Hong Ngoc Hotel. The first morning, I bought flowers from a bicycle peddler in the street. Around the corner, I found Tan My, a silk and embroidery shop run by three generations of Vietnamese women. Then, caught in the spell of French Vietnam, I kept walking, even though I'd only gone out for flowers.

The sign for the tailor on Hang Trong Street reads *Aux Ciseaux de Dop*. Peddlers sell freshly baked baguettes on the curb, and painters set up easels by the bridge leading to Ngoc Son Pagoda on Hoan Kiem Lake. At Fanny, an ice cream shop on the west side of the lake, the nougat glacé is almost as creamy as at Berthillon on the Ile St. Louis in Paris.

Cars and motorcycles tear through seemingly impassable streets, weaving around bicycle taxis, known as *pousses-pousses*. Wherever major arteries intersect, the traffic is every bit as chaotic as around the Étoile in Paris.

The beguiling character of the Old Quarter is partly a product of Hanoi's swampy terrain, pockmarked by lakes fed by the soupy Red River. Even after the lakes were drained, roads that once circled them remained in a grid-defying tangle.

Every street is devoted to a different kind of merchandise, according to the craftsmen from outlying villages who settled there. Thus, Hang Be Street specializes in shoes, Hang Dong Street makes brass and tin, and on Hang Bac Street artisans carve gravestones.

Long, narrow tube houses, some of which stretch as far back from the street as 180 feet, became a feature of the district in precolonial times, but the French encouraged their building in stone and concrete instead of more flammable wood. Often picturesquely dilapidated, the facades have green shutters, iron grillwork, and plaster medallions. Across from the Café des Arts, a bistro on Ngo Bao Khanh Street with credible French onion soup, I saw a tube house restored to its former dignity, but painted hallucinogenic orange.

My favorite part of the Old Quarter was the area around Hanoi's St. Joseph's Cathedral, a Vietnamese administrative center before the French arrived. The examination ground where scholars vied for civil service posts that gained them entry into the ruling mandarin class was nearby, and at 13-17 Cham Cam Street, I found the colonial-era home of Charles

Lagisquet, architect of the Hanoi Opera. Handsomely restored, with a gate, garden, and yellow facade, the villa is now the Spanish Embassy.

The cathedral is approached along leafy Nha Tho Street, lined by cafés, shops, and hotels that cater to Westerners. Halfway down the block, an alley leads to Ba Da Temple, where the devout light tapers to Sakyamuni Buddha and French priests had to hide when Black Flag guerillas, who harassed colonists, laid siege to the neighborhood in 1883.

French missionaries led the way to Vietnam, among them Pierre Pigneau de Behaine, who took little Vietnamese Prince Canh to Versailles to meet Louis XVI. The men of god planted seeds of Catholicism that prospered—today there are some 6 million Catholics in Vietnam—even if the bare condition of the Hanoi Cathedral doesn't reflect it. When I visited the soulful, dingy grey neo-Gothic church, which opened in December 1886, little girls in red and yellow *ao dais* were practicing for a Christmas pageant.

By about 1905, Hanoi was the Paris of Vietnam, a playground for colonists enriched by the rice, rubber, and opium trades. At the same time, it reflected the French Empire's *grande mission civilisatrice*, an effort to shine the golden light of French culture in dark corners of the world. As proof of their altruism, colonists could point to the new bridge over the Red River, street lights, an electric tram, a railroad reaching Haiphong on the coast, and schools where Vietnamese girls and boys learned to write their native language in Roman letters, a transcription system developed by French missionary Alexandre de Rhodes.

Some of the brightest native children continued their educations in the motherland and returned home more French than the French, while others studied Rousseau and joined the revolution. Ho Chi Minh, who lived in Paris from 1917 to 1923 and went on to become the father of Communist Vietnam, said that while the French in France were good, French colonists were cruel and inhuman.

When I moved from the Hong Ngoc to the Metropole Hotel in Hanoi's French Quarter on the southeast side of the lake, I walked in the well-heeled shoes of the colonists Ho hated—second sons, soldiers, priests, and businessmen who hoped to fare better abroad than they had in the old country. The women commanded legions of servants and sat in front of fans smoking opium-laced cigarettes. The men wore white suits and Panama hats, drank cognac and soda, and traveled in touring cars like the vintage Citroens parked at the *porte cochère* of the Metropole.

Even more than the beautifully preserved opera house down the block, the Hotel Metropole epitomizes French Indochina. When it opened in 1901, it was one of the most luxurious hotels in Asia, attracting Charlie Chaplin and Paulette Goddard on honeymoon; Graham Greene, author of *The Quiet American*, a 1955 novel set during the waning days of French Indochina; and a host of American lefties, including Joan Baez, who had to retreat to a bunker during US bombing raids in 1972.

By the time foreign correspondent Stanley Karnow saw the hotel during the American war in Vietnam, it was a horrible specter. "Paint flaked from the ceilings, its bathroom fixtures leaked and rats scurried around its lobby," Karnow wrote in his Pulitzer Prize-winning *Vietnam: A History*.

Today, the Metropole is again the pride of Hanoi, thanks to a restoration in 1990. The three-story lobby yields to a chain of intimate sitting rooms done in dark wood, vintage prints, chinoiserie furniture, orchids, and silk. An Oriental runner lines the creaky grand staircase leading up to rooms in the oldest, most desirable section of the hotel. My chamber reflected the Metropole's glory days in every detail. It had a wood-floored entryway, elegant sitting area, balconies, and a plush bed, where I rested in the hot afternoon, watching the ceiling fan circle.

Le Beaulieu at the Metropole is considered one of the best French restaurants in Vietnam. But when I heard that its *maitre de cuisine,* Didier Corlou, had recently opened his own restaurant Verticale in a 1930s tube house on the outskirts of the French Quarter, I walked there, met the chef, and reserved a table for dinner. Famous for applying classic French cooking techniques to Vietnamese ingredients many Westerners might not recognize, Corlou cooked for former French President Jacques Chirac. "Like the French," he told me, "the Vietnamese will eat anything."

I let him choose my dinner, a sampling of Verticale's best dishes, from foie gras ravioli in mango juice to Ecuadorian chocolate fondant à la Corlou's French *grandmère*.

After that, I roamed widely in the French Quarter and villa district to the west, stopping at l'Èspace, a cultural center and language school supported by the government of France; the Fine Arts Museum, on Nguyen Thai Hoc Street, with several galleries devoted to the work of early 20th-century Vietnamese painters who learned Western techniques at Hanoi's École Supérieure des Beaux-Arts; and the infamous Hanoi Hilton, where Captain John McCain spent five years after his plane was shot down in 1967.

Hoa Lo Prison, as it is officially called, is a popular stop for American tourists who learn that the medieval-looking stone fortress was built by the French in 1896, chiefly for Vietnamese political prisoners. Chained to wooden bunks in grim cell blocks, they succumbed to scabies, dysentery, and torture. There is even a guillotine, imported from France.

Later, over a slice of quiche lorraine at Kinh Doh, a little French bakery near the Fine Arts Museum, I reminded myself that it is dangerous to romanticize. In Vietnam, farmers unable to pay French taxes lost their land. Opium addiction, encouraged by the colonial administration, was rampant. Military conscription and press gangs enslaved a people with a long love of independence.

Just then, I looked up and saw an autographed photo of Catherine Deneuve, who apparently visited Kinh Doh while filming *Indochine*. I wondered if, like me, the quintessential French beauty had come to love Hanoi. Or did she know all along that the French had landed in no dark corner of the world when they colonized Vietnam?

A MEXICAN FISH STORY

Welcome to the end of the road. If you're going to Sian Ka'an Biosphere Reserve, it stops here, near the tip of a long, skinny peninsula about 100 miles south of Cancun. Scrub jungle encroaches on the village, fishermen wait for the opening of lobster season, the town drunk sleeps it off, dogs bark, flies swarm, flotsam surfaces on the beach, and bread rises in the *panderia*.

That's about it for Punta Allen, which promises nothing to visitors seeking parasailing, shopping, golf, or other Cancun-style diversions. Development, which has crept down the Yucatán coast during the last 10 years and turned stretches of wild beach into a self-styled Maya Riviera, hasn't yet reached Punta Allen. And it isn't likely to soon, because the construction of tourist facilities is strictly limited in the roughly 1.5 million-acre ecological reserve that surrounds the drowsy Mexican village.

If, however, you lust to catch a bonefish with a fly and rod, Punta Allen may be one of the most exciting places on earth.

The bonefish, *Albula vulpes*, is a creature only a fly fisherman could love—small (3 to 8 pounds in this area) and too bony to eat, which is why they're generally pursued on a catch-and-release basis. They populate the shallow, mangrove-fringed flats of Sian Ka'an's 20-square-mile Ascension Bay. The balmy setting makes an appealing change of scenery for fly fishermen used to braving the elements on North American trout streams, but it gives the fish a critical advantage: They are almost impossible to see without the help of polarized sunglasses and the trained eyes of a local guide. And even if your casting is precise, the tricky devils are strong and fast, as people who hook and then lose them are dismayed to discover.

"It's the ultimate trout fishing," says the owner and namesake of Bob Marriott's Fly Fishing Store in Fullerton, California. The travel department at Marriott's store sends anglers to several small resorts in the area between Sian Ka'an and the Belize border. It is one of the best places in the world to fish for bones, together with the Bahamas, Los Roques in Venezuela, the Seychelles, and Christmas Island.

Before heading to Sian Ka'an, I took casting lessons with a fly-fishing instructor at Marriott's. By the pond in a Fullerton park, he showed me how to keep a tight loop in the line and apply power at the end of a cast. It's harder than it looks, a completely clumsy enterprise for a novice, until you get the hang of it. By the end of two lessons, I was making reasonably well-formed casts. Of course, I still had no idea of the complex tactics required to hook and land a bonefish. Nevertheless, my teacher seemed upbeat about my chances, though I could tell he thought it strange for a rookie to go after bones, which, I guess, is like someone who's just learned how to ride a bike entering the Tour de France.

The truth is, I wanted an excuse to visit Punta Allen, which, on a visit to the Yucatán Peninsula 10 years ago, had lodged in my memory as one of the world's great end-of-the-road places. I had taken a VW Bug on the perilously potholed, unpaved 30-mile road that scratches its way down the peninsula, often within sight of both the Caribbean to the east and Ascension Bay to the west, but had turned back when the going got too rough.

The average Cancun vacationer never catches wind of Sian Ka'an and the lost world of jungle, beach, and reef that lies between the Maya coastal ruins of Tulum, about 60 miles south of the international airport, and the Mexico-Belize border. Then, too, the infamous Boca Paila Road to Punta Allen culls out all but the most determined.

"Some people make it some of the time," Manuel Sabido, the office manager of Cuzan Guest House, where I stayed in Punta Allen, told one of the guests. Everyone at the table laughed uproariously, but all the new arrivals had bruised behinds and glazed looks from the drive.

Knowing the road's rigors, I had Sabido book me a transfer to Punta Allen from the airport, where I was met by a beat-up white Chevy Suburban. Pedro, the driver, and his blasé young sidekick, Luis, looked as though they could handle anything, so I kicked back and watched the scenery along Highway 307, which follows the east coast of the Yucatán Peninsula all the way to Belize.

The last time I drove the road, nothing interrupted the low, thick jungle, though the area south of Cancún had just been designated a development zone by the Mexican government. Now there were resort entrances every few miles, all grandiose faux-Maya, attracting Europeans for sun-and-sand package vacations. In Playa del Carmen, I saw new fast-food outlets and shopping malls. Formerly a sleepy village with little more than ferry service to Cozumel, it is now one of the fastest-growing cities in the world.

We passed through Tulum, and then stopped at the reserve entrance to pay for admission. Hotels and houses, ruined by one hurricane or another, sat moldering beside the road. Soldiers assigned to drug smuggling watch along the beach, wearing hot boots and uniforms, hitchhiked along the extenuated peninsula. It had rained recently, turning potholes into swimming pools filled with standing water high enough to reach the Suburban's door handles. Every time we launched through one, Pedro grinned determinedly and Luis laughed. "I like this," he said. "It's an adventure."

About 10 miles into the reserve, we crossed a wooden bridge over the cut near Boca Paila Fishing Lodge, where Pedro pointed out a manta ray undulating by a stanchion and a roseate spoonbill stalking fish on a flat. The lodge there is one of the more upscale of about half a dozen around Ascension Bay, and the place where bonefishing was introduced to the area about a decade ago, just as lucrative spiny lobster harvests seemed to be falling off.

Once the gray ghosts—as bonefish became known—were discovered here, North American fly-fishing experts came south to teach Punta Allen lobstermen and lodge guides the tricks of the trade. Locals had to learn how to cast and tie flies, and at first thought the whole catch-and-release enterprise crazy, says Sonja Lillvik, who opened Cuzan around 1985 with her partner, Armando López. Now, guiding bone fishermen in the winter and spring is an important source of income for the people of Punta Allen, besides summer harvesting of lobsters, which are coming back.

There, on the tip of a fish hook, is what Sian Ka'an—and other biosphere reserves selected by the United Nations Educational, Scientific and Cultural Organization (UNESCO)—is about: balancing preservation of some of the world's rarest, most biologically diverse places with the need of indigenous populations to survive and prosper.

Sian Ka'an was decreed in 1986 and enlarged in 1994, and now is operated by the Mexican federal parks system, with extensive help from the Amigos de Sian Ka'an, a not-for-profit group created by environmentalist Barbara MacKinnon de Montes, who was born and raised in the United States but is a naturalized Mexican citizen. Although pressure to develop the reserve has been mounting, Mexican parks, along with the Amigos, have instituted a slow-growth plan for Sian Ka'an, emphasizing low-impact ecotourism and limiting the number of hotel rooms to 1,500. "I would prefer not to see any development," MacKinnon says. "But the area is a biosphere reserve and thus sustainable development is an integral part of the management plan."

To that end, MacKinnon's group and other conservationists encourage traditional cottage industries such as honey harvesting and hammock weaving. They support reforestation and crocodile monitoring efforts. And, perhaps most important, they teach some of the more than 800 residents of Sian Ka'an how to serve as ecotourist guides. Catch-and-release fly-fishing fits nicely in the program.

Thankfully, the reserve is, as yet, too rough and off the beaten track to be in imminent danger of overdevelopment.

A third of it is tangled mangrove islets, swamps, and mirror-like flats. Another third is Caribbean coast, looking out to the long reef that borders the Yucatán. The rest is machete-dulling tropical jungle, virtually untrammeled since the time of the Mayans, who left 23 ruins and a streak of proud independence to their descendants in the area.

Bumping around in the back seat, I tried to read a guide-book about the fauna of Sian Ka'an: crocodiles, jaguars, snakes, manatees, tapirs, pumas, leatherback sea turtles, howler monkeys, almost 250 species of birds—including jabiru storks, parrots, toucans, egrets, and flamingos—and all the fish of the bay, reef, and deep. Suddenly, the Suburban came to a stop. We were finally at Cuzan, although by now it was too dark to see anything beyond a large, round, *palapa*-roofed restaurant, where lights glowed and the sand floor invited bare feet.

Inside, I met Cuzan's owner, Sonja, a transplant to the Yucatán from Northern California; the cook José; bartender Ruby, an expert mixer of strong, limey margaritas; and a seren-dipitous collection of guests. I'd half-expected to be the only person staying at the 14-room lodge, but there were eight of us around the dinner table that night, including a California couple who'd driven the road in a little Nissan to tour the bay, two adventurous young Czech backpackers with scant English, and a father and son from Oklahoma who had come, like me, for bonefish.

In that castaway place, we made a surprisingly cosmo-politan group. The woman from California happened to be the daughter of Czech immigrants, so the backpackers had someone to chat with. Sonja talked about her early days in the village at the end of the road, when she learned how to treat shock because the only people who came to Cuzan were ship-wrecked yachters.

Chuck Goldenberg, an endearing septuagenarian who ties flies in his spare time, and his son John, a London busi-nessman, proved something my Marriott casting instructor had told me: You meet a more ethical class of people when fly-fishing, the sort that takes pleasure in the hunt, not the kill. Chuck dreamed of catching bone, tarpon, and permit fish, a fly-fishing grand slam, but he and John had gotten only three small bones and a 24-inch barracuda, and that was by trolling.

While we got to know each other, José delivered one plate after another, starting that night with delicious lentil soup, then the house specialty, grilled lobster tails, and flan for dessert. Everything was cooked in a *palapa* adjoining the dining room, including terrific breakfasts of *huevos rancheros* and French toast made of freshly baked bread from the *panderia*. One afternoon, I saw a huge red snapper suspended outside the kitchen, which showed up on my plate at dinner that night.

It was late by the time we'd scraped our plates and drained our margarita glasses. In pitch black, Sonja led the way to my room, which was actually a blue-hulled houseboat in dry dock under a palm tree, about 10 feet from the water. Sonja said she and Armando never got around to making it seaworthy, so they turned it into the lodge's funkiest suite.

It had easy chairs on the deck and two plywood-lined rooms, one a bath with a sink and shower dispensing hot and cold water. The sleeping chamber had generator-powered electric lights, louvered windows, a cooler of purified water, and a double bed regally draped with mosquito netting. I read by flashlight, slept lightly, and dreamed bizarrely. At night, the wind kicked up, moaning through the palms, and it rained hard off and on. But my little ship weathered the storm, basking in first-day-after-creation sunshine by the time I awoke.

Early that morning, I walked around the village, which was quite spread out. It has a primary school, a basketball court overlooking the water, an open-air church, offices of fishing collectives, and a handful of small shops, all peaceful and good-natured. Even the stray dogs looked healthy. It struck me as a good, safe place to raise a family, although Sonja later said that Punta Allen attracted a strange crew of gringos, including the occasional American felon on the lam.

At breakfast, I met my fishing guide, Carlos, just 31 but with a wise look beyond his years. He had already loaded fishing tackle and a lunch cooler into the boat, which bobbed by the pier. Once he started the quiet four-stroke engine, we shot south, past the lighthouse at the tip of the peninsula and across the mouth of Ascension Bay, banging against big waves all the way. I kept one hand on my hat and the other on my sunglasses, which, besides sun block, were all the gear I needed, because Carlos supplied the rod—a Redington with a 9-weight line—and the flies, Crazy Charlies, and crab patterns.

Soon we were on the wide, placid bay, flying Indiana Jones–style through narrow channels between mangrove islands. Then we got into skinny water, utterly transparent shallows that are one to two feet deep, where bonefish swim in tight V-formations and root, leaving the impressions of their snouts on the bottom. Carlos turned off the motor and stood in the stern, slowly and silently propelling the boat with a pole, his eyes glued on the water. Ten minutes passed. I was watching a heron wade through the mangrove and thinking about an article I'd recently read in *Smithsonian* magazine on the results of experiments that apparently proved fish feel pain.

Then I heard Carlos say, "Bonefish, 12 o'clock, 25 feet."

This was my cue, but I didn't have my rod ready and couldn't see the prey, so the fish escaped. Later I glimpsed a bone as it swam close to the boat in an arcing flash—the aristocrat of the flats, arrogant and unconcerned that anyone would have the temerity to try to catch it. Mostly, though, I cast blind, to Carlos' directions. When I occasionally put the fly where he saw a fish, he motioned for me to stay still, then to strip, a way of pulling the line in with your hands to make the fly spurt across the bottom, like that favorite bonefish delicacy, mantis shrimp.

Once I hooked a small bonefish but lost it because, concentrating on my casting, I was totally unprepared for its power when it tugged back and ran like 10 inches of silver-coated muscle. After lunch—tuna sandwiches, chips, watermelon, and soda—I hooked and lost another.

So it went, all afternoon. The sun disappeared, obscuring the view even for Carlos, then came out again, its rays emanating from a break in the clouds as in a Renaissance painting of Christ's ascension. An osprey soared across the water. Everything seemed silver. I zoned in and out but was never bored, caught up in the drama of bonefishing.

Returning to Punta Allen, cruising past an islet where a thick flock of frigate birds nested, we explored bird-viewing platforms on tangled fingers of mangrove. When we got back, there was time for a walk to the lighthouse, where I saw big spiders weaving webs and bats embarking on nocturnal hunts.

On the second day, I saw three lemon sharks and a 10-foot crocodile in a channel where I'd innocently gone for a swim. This time, Carlos and I occasionally left the boat to wade in the shallows. The muck at the bottom had the consistency of wet cement and our feet sank to our shins. Carlos helped me land a small bonefish, but it didn't really count because he did most of the work. By then I'd basically given up on catching one on my own and was content to see the sights and go snorkeling out on the reef before heading back to Punta Allen.

Near the end of the third day, I was still wading in the flats behind Carlos, my eyes riveted on the surface, looking for "nervous water," as he put it, that signaled the presence of bones.

Suddenly he stopped. "You see?" he whispered.

"No," I said, scanning the water where he pointed.

"Twenty feet, 1 o'clock. Cast now," he said, "but soft."

I lifted the rod back and let the line fly, utterly amazed because suddenly I saw the tight little V-formation of bonefish he'd spotted.

"They're tailing. Wait," Carlos said. "Cast again, shorter."

I did.

"Strip, strip, strip," Carlos said. "Now stop . . ."

The line jerked, then tensed, like a game of tug-of-war.

"You feel?" Carlos asked. "You got him. Let him run."

The fish ran three times to the far side of the flat, but somehow I played it right this time, reeling in with the grip of the rod propped against my hip. After five interminable minutes, Carlos was removing the hook from what he estimated to be a six-pound bonefish. He took a picture while I cradled it in my arms, then released it to make more silver crescents in Ascension Bay.

I hoped that the hurt, if felt, would pass and that the fish, if it could remember, would think of our encounter without regret.

Then I raised my arms and yelled in unadulterated joy.

But it wasn't just the fish. It was the lost and lovely place—Sian Ka'an

Sonja says it's unlikely they'll ever pave the road. I hope she's right.

Part 2

FOOTSTEPS

People in Circleville, Utah, still debate what led hometown boy Butch Cassidy into a life of crime.

At school in Changsha, China, Chairman Mao read books while swimming in the Xiang River.

Federico Fellini found ideas for his films by sketching people on napkins at the Caffè Canova on the Piazza del Popolo in Rome.

You can learn such things by reading, but to see the places where they happened makes it all real: Colette's banquette at the Le Grand Véfour in Paris, René Magritte's cheese shop in Brussels, the Sleeping Beauty castle in Germany that inspired the Brothers Grimm. I've planned whole trips around biographies, especially the plump details in the side notes that have led me to marvelously untrammeled places. I choose people who fascinate for whatever reason, saints and demons equally, and always come home more sympathetic. Places seem to me a seldom-explored facet of character, but after all, the who and the where are intimately conjoined.

I started on this path many years ago by following the route outlined by Robert Louis Stevenson in *Travels with a Donkey in the Cévennes,* to me the model travel book. It was a pilgrimage, really, albeit not a religious one. In the broadest sense, all trips motivated by things we care about are pilgrimages mapped by people who've gone before us. I wouldn't have made much of an explorer; I'd rather follow in the footsteps of Mao or the Brothers Grimm.

❖ 10 ❖

THE TWO GEORGES

One was a convent-bred beauty with melting black eyes who abandoned her husband and ran away to Paris, where she went through lovers like handkerchiefs.

The other, homely and bookish, devoted her prime to theology, and then scandalized Victorian London by living with a married man.

In France and England, they led superficially different lives but were, more profoundly, like two sides of a reversible garment. When they started writing novels—a vocation that eventually made them celebrated touchstones for their era—both took male pseudonyms.

So, it is by plain, straightforward George that we know the Frenchwoman Amandine Aurore Lucile Dudevant (1804–76), a.k.a. George Sand, author of voluminous essays, letters, plays, and novels; and her English counterpart, Mary Ann Evans (1819–80), who signed her extraordinary books "George Eliot."

Like many fiction and travel lovers, I sometimes am compelled to see the places that inspired and shaped great authors. It is a way of expressing appreciation, of better understanding the wise, deep lessons drawn from their novels and lives. So, early one spring, I followed a trail of ink drops to the homes of Sand and Eliot.

Today, Sand's reputation rests as much on her eventful life as on her novels. She thought love should be a matter of passion, not duty, that relationships between husband and wife, mother and child, mentor and protégé were too varied to be scripted by convention.

The same cannot be said of Eliot. She never intended to flout convention, and her *Middlemarch*, published in installments in 1871 and 1872, is widely considered the apogee of the British novel. I first read it in college, captivated by its protagonist, the young gentlewoman Dorothea Brooke, who

69

makes many mistakes while earnestly trying to find the right way to live.

I sought out the Georges in Paris and London, where they broke with their narrow upbringings to become writers. Then I went further afield, to their native landscapes: Sand's beloved house at Nohant, in central France, and Eliot's childhood home near Coventry in England's Midlands. The first is far better preserved than the second, although neither is a major tourist attraction. Finding them required detection and imagination, because time has turned bucolic 19th-century villages into bedroom communities, country lanes into highways, pastures into shopping malls.

Both writers lived through a time of transformation, as industrialization supplanted agriculture and country folk moved to the city. Traveling widely, they saw cultural, political, and technological upheaval firsthand, but took a long, tolerant view of it, believing that what was truly good was bound to endure.

It took the young Sand as long as three days to travel the 180 miles to Paris from Nohant in a horse-drawn carriage. By the time she was middle-aged, she could get there by train and buggy in 24 hours.

I made the trip from Paris to Nohant by car in an afternoon. There was urban sprawl around Orleans, but fields and forests beyond. When I got off the highways, a tracery of country roads led me to Sand's village, a cluster of warm brownstone cottages surrounded by farm fields and overlooked by a Romanesque church. It has a tourist office, a souvenir shop, and an accommodating inn, L'Auberge de la Petite Fadette, named for one of her novels.

Everything here is just as a literary pilgrim would wish it. Heavy drapes, beds with domineering headboards, patterned wallpaper, solid bureaus and cabinets recalling the style of the Second Empire (1852–70), when Sand's friend and admirer Louis Napoleon ruled France as Napoleon III.

The fresh smell and the scratchiness of the towels suggested they had been dried outside on a line. The house aperitif—a flute of sparkling white Vouvray wine with a hint of Benedictine—was delivered to my chamber on a tray decorated with forsythia blossoms.

Meals in front of the fireplace in the old-fashioned dining room were rich and varied evening entertainments. One night, I had the Chopin menu, with shrimp in a pastry shell, then chicken *bonne femme* in wine sauce, local cheeses, and apple *tarte tatin*, served to the strains of a nocturne by the Polish composer who was Sand's lover.

In the seven summers that Frédéric Chopin spent with her at Nohant, he composed half of his oeuvre, basking in Sand's care and encouragement. But the affair that had set Paris gossiping ended acrimoniously in 1847 because of family squabbles, Chopin's hypochondria, and Sand's need to move on.

Sand's walled, 18th-century chateau across the square from the inn, now a historic monument administered by the French government, can be toured. The writer was raised here by her grandmother after the death of her father, a dashing army officer, and desertion by her mother, a pretty camp follower. Later, Sand lived in the house with her husband, Baron Casimir Dudevant, a country gentleman who preferred hunting to music, art, and literature. The marriage dissolved in 1836 over the boorish manner of Dudevant's philandering and his wife's growing belief that women should enjoy the same sexual freedom as men.

For the rest of Sand's life, the house was a music- and laughter-filled refuge, where the novelist worked, entertained, and raised her son, Maurice, by Dudevant, and her daughter, Solange, generally assumed to have been fathered by Sand's first lover, Jules Sandeau.

Two cedar trees, planted for each of her children, frame the front entrance of the gracious two-story house. It is surrounded by stables, lawns, gardens, and a romantically overgrown park.

In bosky dells here, Sand trysted with Sandeau, a handsome young man from the nearby town of La Châtre, with whom she wrote a novel published in 1831 under the collective pseudonym "J. Sand." She spent much of that year with Sandeau in Paris, where she wore men's clothes, developed a taste for cigars, and found a publisher for another book, written on her own.

The acclaimed *Indiana*, about an unhappily married woman jilted by her lover, was the first novel to appear under the name George Sand. Inside the house, visitors see the boudoir where she wrote *Indiana* and the kitchen where she made preserves, a task as serious, she said, as writing a book. In the salon, she entertained a stream of neighbors, relatives, and famous guests, including composer Franz Liszt, novelist Gustave Flaubert, and painter Eugene Delacroix. She turned one room into a theater, where her plays and puppet shows were staged.

As Sand aged, she devoted herself to her grandchildren and wrote many of the 20,000 letters that show off her fluid style at its best. Habitually clad in a black mantilla, she looked increasingly like Queen Victoria.

By the time of her peaceful death at age 72, in the blue canopy bed upstairs, she had reversed her views on the role of women, who she thought were too ill-educated to vote and fit only for marriage and motherhood, and had become a thickly varnished feature in the world of French letters.

I was happy to discover that one could still follow walking paths from one village to the next, as Sand did when visiting friends. She used the 15th-century fortress in nearby St.-Chartier as the setting for *The Master Pipers*, and La Chatre has a small museum with a room dedicated to her.

Sand also spent considerable time in Paris, occupying more than 25 apartments in the course of her life. One was in the hilly Ninth Arrondissement on the Square d'Orleans, a fashionable address for writers and artists at the time. Nearby, on the rue Chaptal, the Musée de la Vie Romantique displays plentiful Sand memorabilia, including a model of her elegant hand.

Sand rests in the family cemetery at Nohant, her tomb decorated with floral tributes from admirers.

Fewer devotees visit Eliot's grave in Highgate Cemetery, a few Tube stops north of central London. When I paid my respects, there was only a gardener, with an annoying weed whacker.

The neo-Gothic cemetery, founded in 1839, is full of weeping stone angels, overgrown woods, and mossy headstones leaning on one another like old friends. I was delighted to find that the novelist rests beside her dear friend and companion, George Henry Lewes, who first encouraged her to write fiction. He negotiated book deals for her, kept negative criticism away from her oversensitive eyes, and gave her the George half of her nom de plume. The Eliot half was plucked out of thin air, "a good mouth-filling, easily pronounceable word," the novelist said.

After my visit to Highgate Cemetery, I headed north for Eliot country. Her Midlands family disowned her in 1854 when she went to live with Lewes, a believer in free love who had condoned his wife's liaison with another man, thereby abnegating his right to divorce her. Thus outcast and settled in London with Lewes—a devoted married couple in all but name—the writer could go home only in her imagination.

It takes about two hours to drive from London to the Midlands, much of which is now uninterrupted urban sprawl. But you can still see the spire of Holy Trinity Church in central Coventry, where Eliot lived in her dour, spinsterish 20s, ministering to her ailing, widowed father. She was befriended by a group of freethinkers there, read books that debunked the Bible, and ultimately renounced organized religion.

Solidly working-class Nuneaton, where Eliot spent her youth, is about 10 miles north, with streets lined by rows of attached terraced housing and pubs named for her novels, such as the *Felix Holt* in the marketplace.

There used to be a statue of Nuneaton's famous daughter nearby, but when I visited, it had been taken away for repair after a truck backed into it.

Scholars do research in the Eliot archive at the Nuneaton library, and a pretty park in the center of town bears her name. There is a museum with a gallery devoted to Eliot, where visitors can see her piano and writing desk.

Her father was the estate agent for Arbury Hall, outside Nuneaton. She was born in a cottage there, but the family soon moved to Griff House, an eight-bedroom Georgian farmhouse on Nuneaton-Coventry Road, surrounded by 280 acres of fields, gardens, and orchards. For more than 20 years, Griff and its environs were Eliot's world, the remembered-from-a-distance setting for her first fiction, *Scenes of Clerical Life*, published in 1858.

Alas, Griff is now a steakhouse and motel on a busy roundabout. A wing of chockablock rooms has been added, and from the window in the attic where Eliot played as a girl, the view is of fast-food eateries and industrial estates. Traces of the original building are apparent only in the southern facade and flagstone entrance.

There, I met Bill and Kathleen Adams, chairman and secretary of the George Eliot Fellowship, respectively. They have served at the organization's helm for almost 40 years, organizing literary luncheons, laying wreaths on Eliot memorials, and helping biographers. Several times a year, they lead bus tours of Eliot country, giving aficionados the chance to see important outlying sites related to the writer, such as Arbury Hall.

The stately Gothic revival mansion, surrounded by a 4,000-acre estate, is the home of Viscount and Viscountess Daventry, open to the public infrequently during the spring and summer. But the Adamses had obtained permission to show me around the grounds, which are carpeted with bluebells in the spring. We stopped outside the library where Eliot was allowed to read and drove past South Farm, her birthplace.

The Adamses also took me to Chilvers Coton church in the Nuneaton suburbs, where Eliot worshiped as a girl. Along the way, they quoted pertinent passages from her books and reminded me that, despite her controversial private life, she was admired by the straight-laced Queen Victoria.

Later, I went for a walk in the countryside north of Nuneaton, where I met an old man with a dog who might have stepped out of *Middlemarch*. I followed a dirt lane over Coventry Canal and some train tracks, evidence of technological development that changed life and the landscape in her time, even as it changes ours now. But I felt less bothered by it, because I could, at last, feel Eliot's presence in the smell of freshly turned earth, in the grazing sheep, and in the old man patting his dog and saying, "Come on, mate. Let's go home."

Sand and Eliot were right; good things may not be easy to find, but they endure.

❖ ❖

❖ 11 ❖

COLETTE'S GHOST

A frizzy-haired old woman wearing sandals used to sit on a stoop at the Palais-Royal in Paris. If people took her for a tramp what did she care? Her extraordinary life was almost over. Now she could spend her afternoons eyeing passersby and cooing to stray cats.

Her ghost still haunts the quiet north arcade of the Palais-Royal, only now there's a plaque to identify her: *Colette spent her last years at the edge of this garden.* It doesn't give her dates; vain to the last, she wouldn't have liked that. But when she died at 81 in 1954, she received a state funeral in the palace's *Cour d'honneur.* Her coffin lay under a French tricolor, surrounded by wreaths, and thousands came to pay their respects.

Colette has gone in and out of style, but by any measure, she was a great writer, the author of 80 books, including five novels about the insouciant teenage girl Claudine that were all-time French bestsellers, inspiring two plays, a shirt collar, perfume, candy, and cigarettes. Ten of her works were made into films, most famously, the 1958 musical *Gigi*.

And then there was Colette, the woman, whose life arced across one of the most fascinating periods in French history, from the ebullient Belle Epoque to the German Occupation. For half a century, she scandalized *le tout Paris*, lopping off her long schoolgirl braid and varnishing her toenails, gallivanting around town in an apparent ménage à trois with her husband and his girlfriend, cross-dressing for her lesbian lover, baring her breasts on stage, divorcing, remarrying, and seducing her teenage stepson.

Whenever she hit the rocks, Colette remade herself, resulting in a CV that reads like the Yellow Pages: journalist, critic, pornographer, music hall performer, lecturer, screenwriter, advice columnist, beautician (though her aging looks were no advertisement for her skills).

A naturally liberated woman, Colette despised feminists. She ate gluttonously and got fat; loved animals but monstrously ignored her only daughter; saved her Jewish third husband from World War II concentration camps while earning a living writing for the Nazi-controlled press.

Every insult you can throw at Colette sticks. In spite—or maybe *because*—of that, she earned plaques that mark her passage all over France.

I found the one at the Palais-Royal by chance when I was living in Paris; I then started reading her work, which came as a revelation. In her best books—*The Pure and the Impure, The Cat, The Ripening Seed*—she probed the perversities of the human heart with the minimalist delicacy of a poet and a discriminating contrarianism I've come to think of as essentially French.

Secrets of the Flesh, Judith Thurman's masterful 1999 biography, tells the story of Colette's long, lush life. But traveling is how I come to understand the things I care about, so I tried to raise Colette's ghost by following her footsteps in France, the first of them taken in the Burgundian village of St. Sauveur-en-Puisaye.

St. Sauveur-en-Puisaye is a straight shot about one hundred miles south of Paris along the A6. But once I turned off the highway I got lost, as I always do on little roads in the countryside—*la France profonde*, as they call it—where seeds are more important than the style of shoes. St. Sauveur-en-Puisaye is nowheresville, France, north of Burgundy wine country and the great Romanesque abbey church at Vézelay, a stonily silent village in any event, but especially so when I found it on a weekday afternoon in March, cold sunshine coaxing forsythia into early bloom. The streets were empty except for three children whom I asked for directions. They huddled for a minute, and then led me on their bikes to the bed and breakfast inn where I'd booked a room.

Colette called the region "poor Burgundy." But it has wide-open fields, forests, lakes, and other charms she well knew and rendered in two beautiful memoirs. *Sido* and *My Mother's House* are thus recommended reading for Colette pilgrims, glowing recollections of a seamlessly happy childhood and the woman who gave it to her.

Her mother Sidonie—known as Sido—was a propertied widow with two children, a good French *bourgeoisie* by all appearances. But the heart of a bohemian beat inside her corset. When her first husband died, she married for love the second time, choosing the quiet oddball Jules-Joseph Colette, a veteran who lost a leg in one of Napoleon III's wars.

Born in 1873, their youngest child, Sidonie-Gabrielle, was raised with encompassing love and surprising license. She was left free to roam in the woods, tag along after her two older brothers, play with a pack of friends in the ruined chateau at the top of the village, and take books by Balzac and Zola down from the top shelves to be devoured with the imperfect understanding of a prepubescent girl.

Empty and for sale, the family home on rue de l'Hospice (now rue Colette) has battened-up shutters and a dour stone facade. As the writer recalled, it "smiled only on its garden side," in back, where the little girl nested in the grass while Sido gardened.

A passage from *My Mother's House* made Colette's childhood vivid to me. In it, the writer recalls moving from her cubbyhole upstairs near Sido's bedroom to a chamber downstairs. Late one night, consumed with worry about being separated by a flight of steps from her cherished daughter, Sido carried the sleeping child back upstairs. Colette woke the next morning in her old bed, confused, and ran to tell her mother that she'd been abducted.

The village also evokes Colette's alter ego: wicked and wonderful Claudine from St. Sauveur, known in the author's first books as Montigny, where the heroine attends a school full of precocious Lolitas, run by a lesbian headmistress. In its prototype (now the town hall), I saw the classroom where the writer studied geography, learned to sew, and pulled pranks.

Apart from the books, the best place to get to know the writer is the Colette Museum, housed in a 17th-century chateau on the hill above town. Its thoughtfully designed galleries contain art, photos, and memorabilia any Colette fan would consider treasures: the Palais-Royal bedroom suite where the invalid writer spent her last years; posters from her music hall career; pictures of her pets; and a room dedicated to her daughter with the journalist-statesman Henry de Jouvenel, another Colette, nicknamed "Bel Gazou," who donated much of the material in the museum.

After Colette left St. Sauveur at 20, she rarely returned, and the buttoned-up village took no pride in her louche celebrity. It's said that, once, when she did go back for the installation of a plaque on her house, townsfolk attended the ceremony with rocks in their pockets, though thankfully they restrained themselves from hurling them at the harlot.

To my mind, if anyone earned Old Testament punishment, it was her first husband, Henri Gauthier-Villars, a Paris music critic who signed his squibs "Willy." His voracious sexual appetite inclined toward young actresses and prostitutes. At the time, the French capital had a population of about 3 million, including 100,000 girls who worked the boulevards, as well as grand courtesans like Manet's Olympia and Zola's Nana. In Montmartre bars and shady spots in the Bois de Boulogne, a lesbian subculture thrived, though cross-dressing in public was forbidden by hypocritical French law.

When the blushing bride set out for Paris in 1893 with Willy, she left her innocence and illusions behind.

He took her to his Left Bank bachelor pad above the family publishing firm. But Venusberg, as Willy called it, was cramped and clearly unsuitable for a newly married couple. So they moved to a nearby third-floor apartment at 28 rue Jacob, marked by another Colette plaque, a few doors down from the famous Paris patisserie Ladurée.

Colette's deflowering was completed there, followed by her discovery that Willy had a mistress. Shattered, she took to bed—

suffering from venereal disease, she later claimed—but soon rose to the challenge of her new life, exploiting her androgynous looks by appearing at parties in a sailor's suit, entertaining Willy's paramours in the apartment, and eventually sharing one of them with him, a liaison salaciously rendered in the third Claudine novel.

It was during their time on rue Jacob that Willy suggested she write down some of her childhood memories, which he consigned to a bottom desk drawer. Only later, when the couple had moved to a new place on the Right Bank, did he reconsider the notebooks and ask for a bit of elaboration.

"Couldn't you warm this up a bit?" Colette has him saying in *My Apprenticeship*, her 1936 memoir.

Claudine at School took Paris by storm when it was published under Willy's name in 1900. He held the copyright, which he later sold for a song, earning Colette's undying animosity. Still, Willy served as improbable midwife to the first Claudine, which remains a beguiling read—either as stylish soft porn or as a harbinger of deeper works to come.

After rue Jacob, Colette lived at a dozen different addresses during her six decades in Paris. I could not see all of them, but I did track down one of two apartments on stuffy, very Right Bank rue des Courcelles where Willy and Colette spent the last years of their marriage. Nothing about the ramrod-straight avenue, part of Baron Haussmann's late 19th-century redesign of Paris, bears witness to her time there, but Colette fans will recognize nearby Parc Monceau as the setting of a poignant scene from *Claudine in Paris* in which the heroine encounters her old girlfriend Luce, who has become the kept woman of an aging "uncle."

By the time Colette and Willy divorced in 1905, she had a new lover, a French marquise known as Missy, part of a small, select group of rich Paris lesbians, whom she met performing in an amateur theatrical. Though her Sapphic phase did not last long, it inspired her to go into show business, acting silent movie–style in risqué skits like *Rêve d'Égypte*, which opened at the Moulin Rouge in 1907.

The famous old Montmartre theater is a bus tourist trap

now, especially tawdry in full daylight. But a plaque there mentions the riot incited by *Rève d'Égypte*, a sketch about an archaeologist, played by an actress in obvious drag, who falls in love with a mummy, played by Colette in a spangled brassiere. When they kissed on the lips, the house exploded.

After that—through two world wars and two more husbands—Colette never left the limelight. Willing to do anything to support herself as a writer, she lectured, promoted silly products, and acted in forgettable plays based on her novels. Maybe she lived too long and became a cliché. But a generation of younger writers, including Sartre and Cocteau, eventually discovered her; the prestigious Académie Goncourt and French Légion d'Honneur recognized her literary achievement; a gold nameplate identifies her favorite banquette at the restaurant Le Grand Véfour; and Paris now has a Place Colette next to the Comédie Francaise.

When she finally died of myriad disorders connected to self-indulgence and old age, she was laid to rest in the company of other luminaries at Père Lachaise cemetery. It was raining on the afternoon I went to pay my respects at the marble slab that marks her grave—her last plaque, if you will.

But I don't think she's there. I think she's still at the Palais-Royal, contemplating mischief.

12

FINDING FELLINI

He was 18 and inexperienced—in all respects—when he came to Rome in 1938. For Federico Fellini, it was the beginning of a love affair that lasted more than 50 years.

Rome dazzled and indulged him. It fed the dreams he turned into such movies as *La Dolce Vita, 8 1/2, Roma,* and others so imaginative that a word had to be coined to describe them: "Fellini-esque." He could hardly bear to be anywhere but Rome, even when Hollywood summoned him to receive an Oscar (four for Best Foreign Film and an honorary award in 1993, just a few months before his death).

"When I was a boy, I wanted to travel and see the world," he told Charlotte Chandler, the author of reminiscences titled *I, Fellini,* "but then I found Rome and found my world."

The 10th anniversary of the director's death was marked in 2003 with "Romacord Fellini," a celebration that included concerts, presentations, and showings of the master's films. I went in October for the festivities and to see Rome through Fellini's eyes, to sit in his favorite cafes and wander past the places in his films that had lodged in my imagination: the Colosseum at night, lighted up like a birthday cake, as in *Roma*; the Bernini colonnade at St. Peter's Square, where an errant young wife is reconciled with her husband at the end of *The White Sheik*; and, above all, Trevi Fountain, which some aficionados cannot conjure without envisioning Anita Ekberg and Marcello Mastroianni of *La Dolce Vita* wading in it.

To prepare for the trip, I spent most of my free nights for about a month watching videos: *La Strada* (1954), *Nights of Cabiria* (1957), *La Dolce Vita* (1960), *8 1/2* (1963), *Satyricon* (1969), *Roma* (1972), *Amarcord* (1974). Bizarre, vulgar, illogical, brimming with psychological disorder, Fellini's films don't submit easily to interpretation. Loving them is a visceral thing, a little like his love for Rome.

"FeFe," Roman taxi drivers used to call to him, using the nickname by which he was known around the city, "why don't you make pictures we can understand?" He says in *I, Fellini*, "I answer them that is it because I tell the truth, and the truth is never clear, while lies are quickly understood by everyone."

It seems as though all of Rome knew Fellini. I met some of his old friends and colleagues almost effortlessly while I was there: Luigi Esposito, retired concierge at the Grand Hotel Plaza, who knew Fellini when he was sketching American GIs on the streets of the city to make money during World War II; and photographer Carlo Riccardi, who used to run into Fellini around town while taking pictures of people living the sweet life before Fellini's film taught us to call it *La Dolce Vita*.

"He was a lovely man," Esposito said. "Even when he was young, he was something."

Fellini was tall and skinny when he came to Rome from his hometown of Rimini, too ashamed to wear swimming trunks at the beach in the nearby seaside town of Fregene, where he later bought a house and is remembered with an annual film festival.

In his imagination, he looked more like suave, sexy Mastroianni, whom he cast as the lead in such autobiographical films as *8 1/2*. The director filled out and adopted accessories—tweed hat, brim turned down, and a coat, collar turned up—that created a look for him. As he aged, his eyebrows remained dark when his hair turned gray, and his *bella figura* increased in girth because he couldn't resist pasta and pastry.

I frequently felt his presence. Walking the Pincio, a park on the northwest side of Rome, I fancied I saw him and his wife of 50 years, actress Giulietta Masina, on a dignified afternoon *passeggiata*. At the window of a shoe store on via della Croce near the Spanish Steps, I wondered what FeFe would think of a certain pair of boots.

This section of Rome, stretching from about the Spanish Steps to the Piazza del Popolo, was Fellini's neighborhood. He used to have coffee at Canova, a stylish cafe on the Piazza del Popolo, which he is said to have preferred to adjacent Caffe Rosati because Canova's sidewalk tables were shaded from the morning sun.

Sandwiched between these, one on each side of the via del Corso, are the almost-twin Baroque churches of Santa Maria dei Miracoli and Santa Maria di Montesanto, designed in the 1660s by Carlo Rainaldi. Santa Maria del Popolo is across the way, justly more renowned for its two Caravaggios depicting the crucifixion of St. Peter and the conversion of St. Paul, intimate images that serve to remind us that, unlike many directors, Fellini took his inspiration from painting, not literature.

The piazza at the churches' doorsteps is a terrific, wide-open space, centered by an Egyptian obelisk, with steps leading up to a breathtaking overlook in the Pincio. The view of Rome from there is almost as good as in the opening scene of *La Dolce Vita*, which follows a helicopter carrying a statue of Jesus Christ over the Eternal City, dangling from a cable as if it were a toy action figure.

An excellent sampling of Roman humanity rushes across the Piazza del Popolo in plain view of an espresso drinker at Canova. "The show [in Italy] can be so engrossing that many people spend most of their lives just looking at it," Luigi Barzini writes in *The Italians*. Fellini was a great people watcher and collector; people-watching stimulated his thinking about the characters in his films. He often drew people who interested him on napkins and tablecloths—fat, ugly, grizzled, dwarfish, the odder the better, and, if female, magnanimously endowed.

Along with filmmaking, pasta, the circus, and dreams, women are what Fellini adored most. It was part Italian machismo, part rebellion against the Catholic faith in which he was raised, and part mother love, as evidenced by his fascination with big breasts. Fellini's sexism struck me as more sexy than sexist, a quality often missed by tourists flocking to the chaste Vatican and the Forum.

I felt it all around his neighborhood, where some of Rome's ritziest shops are clustered. On via del Babuino, near Fellini's apartment, a woman can buy a negligee to match her sheets, and on chic via dei Condotti, running from the foot of the Spanish Steps to via del Corso, there are costly gifts for lovers from La Perla, Max Mara, Dolce & Gabbana. In *I, Fellini*, the director tells author Chandler something that echoed in my mind about rich men taking their mistresses shopping there in the afternoon: "After that, they go to the 'nest,' and the man is finished in time to arrive home for dinner with his wife and children."

Regardless of where he'd been, Fellini went home to elfish Giulietta, his soul mate and muse. Her performance in *La Strada* as the heart-rending clown Gelsomina, opposite a savage circus strongman played by Anthony Quinn, helped make Fellini famous. He loved the privacy of their life together. In his brief 1993 Oscar acceptance speech, he brought down the house by saying, "Thank you, dearest Giulietta. And please, stop crying." At the end of his funeral in Michelangelo's church of Santa Maria degli Angeli, near the Piazza della Repubblica, she did the same, waving and saying simply, "Ciao, amore." She died of cancer five months later.

They lived at No. 110 via Margutta, marked by a simple plaque, on a pretty Roman lane close to the Piazza del Popolo. Artists and antiques dealers have long favored this street, which has a few restaurants and hotels but is otherwise residential.

Nearby, the Grand Hotel Plaza on via del Corso, where I stayed for several nights, is another stop for Fellini pilgrims. From his childhood, the director was in awe of grand hotels where beautiful rich people drank champagne. With a fabulously frescoed inner lobby and marble staircase guarded by a large stone lion, the Plaza evokes Fellini's majestic hotel fantasies.

My room on the third floor was pure Italian baronial. There were prints of Rome on the walls, tassels, fringed lamps, a generous double bed, and flowingly draped casement windows, all with the look of a beautiful Roman woman of a certain age who's barely hanging on to her looks.

When Fellini found fame, he could afford to entertain American producers here. "They spend their days sitting in their underpants in the biggest suites making long-distance calls," he says in *I, Fellini*. "When they receive you . . . they make no effort to put on anything more."

Fellini found shooting on location hard to control and had elaborate re-creations of famous Roman monuments—Trevi Fountain, for instance—created at Cinecittà, the studio on the southern outskirts of the city that became virtually synonymous with him. It isn't easy for Fellini fans to visit the places where key scenes from his movies were filmed.

But you can take the Metropolitana from Piazza del Popolo to Cinecittà, as he routinely did. He went there even when he wasn't making a picture to get inspiration and feed the studio's stray cats.

Riding the subway is a Fellini-esque trip in itself, evoking an unforgettable sequence in *Roma*, the director's paean to the Eternal City, depicting the construction of the Metropolitana. In it, workers break through a wall underground and discover an ancient Roman house with breathtakingly intact wall frescoes, like those tourists see at the National Roman Museum in the Palazzo, that melt away before our horrified eyes.

Flush times didn't last, and Cinecittà moldered; eventually part of it was sold to developers of Cinecittà Due, a big shopping mall. But somewhere FeFe is smiling because in the decade after his death, Cinecittà came back to life, attracting American movie projects again, including Martin Scorsese's *Gangs of New York* and Mel Gibson's *The Passion of Christ*.

Beyond Cinecittà, Canova, via Margutta, and the Grand Hotel Plaza, Fellini devotees must rely on the imagination to guide them. For summoning up *La Dolce Vita*, a movie that fascinated and repulsed viewers, visits to via Veneto and the Trevi Fountain are musts.

The Veneto fell on hard times in the 1980s and 1990s, but swank idlers once again fill Harry's Bar, Doney, and the Cafe de Paris. And crowds never forsook the 18th-century Baroque fountain, a looming, white-marble confection with water so clear and inviting that some people can't resist plunging in à la Ekberg and Mastroianni.

Just off the little piazza, on Vicolo delle Bollette, is Al Moro, a trattoria favored by Fellini, known for its version of spaghetti alla carbonara. The director liked proprietor Mario Romagnoli's face, which appears in a large photograph in the front room, and cast him in *Satyricon*.

One night, I took a taxi to Trastevere, on the west side of the Tiber River, to tour the International Museum of Film and Entertainment, a funny little place on via Portuense, way off the beaten track, which tries its best to live up to its name. It is stuffed with Italian film, TV, and theater memorabilia, including scripts and letters written by Fellini.

Then, in a flash of enlightenment, I knew what next to do to celebrate Fellini. I saw a movie at the Alcazar, one of the many theaters in Trastevere: Bernardo Bertolucci's *The Dreamers*, about a youthful ménage a trois, which I found ultimately tiresome. It didn't matter, though. I was in a bigger, better motion picture: Fellini's Rome.

13

BUTCH AND SUNDANCE

"Most of what follows is true."

That's the opening of *Butch Cassidy and the Sundance Kid*, the 1969 movie about two bandits born as the sun was setting over the mesas and buttes of the old Wild West.

Morally ambiguous, violent, a classic western turned inside-out, the movie struck a chord with Vietnam War–era audiences who stood and cheered when Paul Newman as Butch and Robert Redford as Sundance met a hail of bullets in a dusty Bolivian town, etching the final freeze frame onto my 15-year-old heart.

I didn't know it then, but the movie wrote something else there: a love of sumptuous Western scenery, like the kind you see in Utah. Only part of the movie was filmed there, and the real Butch robbed banks and trains all across the West, making frequent stops at Fanny Porter's high-class bordello in San Antonio. But with five national parks, Utah's scenic grandeur is unrivaled in North America, and it's also where Robert LeRoy Parker, alias Butch Cassidy, was born in 1866.

On the Parker spread in the beautiful Sevier River Valley, 200 miles south of Salt Lake City, Butch learned to be a cowboy first, and, later, how to put his brand on other peoples' livestock. He trained his mounts not to shy at the sound of gunfire and to stand still when he jumped into the saddle from behind. Apparently, he pulled only one big job in his home state, the 1897 Pleasant Valley Coal Co. payroll robbery at Castle Gate.

But between heists, he and his Wild Bunch gang often hid out in isolated nooks and crannies on Utah's Colorado Plateau.

I set out to track the historical and Hollywood outlaw in Utah, but got only as far as St. George when I started running into a third persona: the apocryphal Butch, who is in some ways the most interesting because of the people who told me about him.

Sprawling St. George is the capital of Utah's Dixie, so named because Mormon church leaders dispatched pioneers like Butch's father, Maximillian Parker, to settle and propagate cotton there around the time of the Civil War.

Downtown, at the Washington County Library, I met bear-sized Bart Anderson, widely known as Ranger Bart because he has devoted his golden years to giving slide shows at nearby national and state parks.

The one on Butch is the most popular in his repertoire. It features some well-known vintage photos of the outlaw, including the mug shot taken when he was sent to the Wyoming Territorial Penitentiary for horse stealing in 1894 and a group portrait of the Wild Bunch dressed like city slickers. That picture, thought to have been taken in 1900, was proudly displayed in the window of a Fort Worth photography studio. When law enforcement officials spotted it, they used it to create wanted posters.

The Butch it portrays is a handsome, affable-looking man with a mischievous smile beneath his mustache. By many accounts, he charmed locals and lawmen, paid a penniless widow's mortgage, rode back for his dog in the middle of an escape, and never took a man's life (though his Wild Bunch henchman Harvey Logan, a.k.a. Kid Curry, is often remembered as a psychopathic killer).

"Butch was a contagious fellow, well-liked," Anderson said. "The movie got that much right."

But interviews with scores of people revealed what Anderson considers fallacies in William Goldman's Oscar-winning screenplay: Elzy Lay was the real brains of the gang. The relationship between Butch and Sundance's girlfriend, Etta Place, played in the movie by Katharine Ross, was far from platonic. And, as many locals claim, Butch didn't die in South America on November 6, 1908. Instead, he and Sundance rode all the way back to Utah, stopping in Mexico to meet Pancho Villa.

Others have tried to prove the opposite, including writer Anne Meadows. In her book *Digging Up Butch and Sundance*, she marshals documentary evidence about the movements of Butch, Sundance, and Etta after they fled the United States in 1901, and reports on the inconclusive exhumation of a grave thought to contain the remains of the outlaws in the village of San Vicente, Bolivia.

The movie takes a middle ground by leaving their fate to the imagination, but it faithfully underscores the passing of the outlaw era in the scene in which Butch takes Etta riding on a bicycle, a newfangled contraption at the time not about to supplant the horse, in his opinion. The scene, set to Burt Bacharach and Hal David's *Raindrops Keep Fallin' on My Head*, was filmed in the ghost town of Grafton on the Smithsonian Butte Road Scenic Backway, a graded dirt road southwest of Zion Canyon National Park.

At the cleaned-up cemetery in Grafton, I found a historic marker and artificial flowers on the hard earth graves of Mormon pioneers. They settled here around 1860, just down the Virgin River from the magnificent red rock cathedrals of Zion Canyon, but floods, disease, and hostile Indians made the colony unsustainable. By 1910, most of them had moved on, leaving Grafton to Hollywood location scouts who found backdrops in southern Utah for a passel of westerns, including *The Deadwood Coach* with Tom Mix (1924), *My Friend Flicka* (1943), and John Ford's *Rio Grande* (1950).

Down the hill, the same historic preservationists who rehabbed the cemetery have fixed up an old Grafton homestead and the schoolhouse that Butch and Etta passed on their bicycle. Cattle still graze in nearby pastures and, of course, the Navajo sandstone cliffs behind the ghost town never needed restoration.

After that, I drove east through the red-and-white slickrock country along Utah 9, then turned north on US 89, another showstopper of a road that runs through the hamlet of

Orderville, where shops sell porcelain dolls and custom-made coffins. In the late afternoon, the lowering sun highlights the edges of the nearby Markagunt and Paunsaugunt plateaus with colors you would never find in a paint box and searches into side canyons for bad guys on the lam.

I turned east on Utah 12, headed for Ruby's Inn, on the threshold of amazing Bryce Canyon, whittled from limestone into a gallery of pinnacles and spires known as "hoodoos." Mormon pioneer Ebenezer Bryce, who gave his name to the landmark that is now a national park, once said, "It's a helluva place to lose a horse."

It would be just as hard to find a horse—or, for that matter, a fugitive from justice—in Red Canyon, an overture to Bryce a few miles west of the national park turnoff. Its Cassidy Trail fingers north into a network of gulches, lined by tangled cedars, scree, hoodoos, and vermilion-colored cliffs, where locals say a posse tracked a teenage Butch when he took up rustling. Bryce Canyon Pines, a nearby motel, offers daylong trail rides to the remains of one of the stone cabins where he is thought to have stashed fresh horses for the Pony Express–style relay escapes he perfected. But with snow on the ground when I was there, all I could do was clamber up the side of Cassidy Draw to ascertain that Butch knew a good hideout when he saw one.

The next day, I drove west to the ranching town of Panguitch, with a main street made wide enough for a wagon to turn around. Its block-long business district has old-fashioned, Western storefronts occupied by cafés and shops, including Cowboy Collectibles, where I found reproductions of Wild Bunch wanted posters.

Panguitch is where Butch's youngest sister, Lula Parker Betenson, spent her last years after writing *Butch Cassidy, My Brother*, published in 1975. The book confounded Western scholars with its assertion that Butch arrived at the Parker home in nearby Circleville in 1925 driving a new black Ford, unscathed by the bullets of *federales* who supposedly had killed him and Sundance in Bolivia.

Lula was just a toddler when her big brother left home, but in the 1930s, she believed widely publicized claims that

William T. Phillips of Spokane, Washington, was Butch. Later, she changed her mind, saying she knew where the real Butch was buried but planned to take the secret to her grave. Ranches, barns, and pastures line the 20-mile stretch of US 89 north of Panguitch. West of the road just before Circleville, I spotted the lonesome, old Parker homestead beside an alfalfa field and a poplar windbreak. It is privately owned, but there was no one to stop me from inspecting the wood cabin with a loft where Butch likely slept as a boy.

I stopped at Butch Cassidy's Hideout restaurant and motel in Circleville for Butch's Special Cheeseburger plate, then visited 84-year-old Alfred Fullmer. Sitting on the couch in his sunny living room, Fullmer remembered racing horses with some of the Parker boys. Like some locals, he believed Lula's story about Butch's 1925 homecoming, though he said no one talked much about the bandit before the movie. "Afterward, everybody claimed they'd seen him. I don't know, maybe I did," Fullmer said with a rueful smile.

The next morning, I headed east on Utah 12, to my mind one of the finest scenic roads in the United States. It makes a 120-mile loop through the minuscule ranching communities of Tropic, Cannonville, and Henrieville at the threshold of 1.9-million-acre Grand Staircase-Escalante National Monument, then rounds the east side of 10,188-foot Powell Point. I drove with one hand on the wheel and the other on my camera all the way to the high desert town of Escalante, where I picked up my friend Bill Wolverton, a ranger for Glen Canyon National Recreation Area, which abuts Grand Staircase-Escalante. He knows the region well and offered to take me for a hike.

On our way to the trailhead for Upper Calf Creek Falls, we stopped at Head of the Rocks Point, overlooking what seemed like the edge of the world. There, Wolverton showed me the north face of the massive Kaiparowits Plateau, the snow-capped Henry Mountains to the northeast, and the badlands around Waterpocket Fold, a hundred-mile-long buckle of earth with a Parthenon frieze of sculptured red-and-white rock marking Capitol Reef National Park.

Utah 12 crosses the wild Escalante River near Boynton

Overlook, named for John Boynton, who turned himself in after killing Washington Phipps in a dispute in 1878. Short of manpower, the Escalante authorities gave him $10 and told him to ride to the county seat in Parowan, about a hundred miles west. Boynton was never seen again.

It was a short walk from the highway to Upper Calf Creek Falls. Wolverton and I sat looking into the canyon, remembering the scene in the film in which Butch and Sundance jump from just such an aerie, yelling a profanity. "I saw that movie again, and it was like 40 years hadn't passed," Wolverton said. "I could anticipate all the lines."

After that, I took a section of Utah 12 over 10,000-foot Boulder Mountain, unpaved until the 1970s, then spent the night in a room with a fireplace at the Lodge at Red River Ranch on the Fremont River west of Torrey, a beautifully restored stagecoach inn that the owners claim Butch visited.

The next morning in Capitol Reef National Park, I hiked nearly two miles up the side of Grand Wash to Cassidy Arch, a spot wild enough to have earned Butch's name, and then went on to Hanksville, about 50 miles east of Capitol Reef. There, I met Utah canyoneer and guidebook writer Mike Kelsey, who had promised to take me to Robbers Roost, a 30-mile-wide mesa banked on the south by the Dirty Devil River. Together with Wyoming's Hole-in-the-Wall and Brown's Hole on the Utah-Colorado border, the roost was the impregnable lair of the Wild Bunch. It had narrow slot canyons for hiding out, some springs, just enough fodder for horses, and overhangs where bandit sentries watched for posses.

It can be reached only on rough, mostly unmarked dirt roads mined with rocks and sand traps. Kelsey, an old hand at such terrain, drove fast, pointing out water tanks for cattle that roam free on land leased by the government to ranchers. Around midmorning, we pulled up at Robbers Roost Spring, in a deep-set gulch rimmed by red rock with water palatable to cows and horses but too bitter for humans.

From there, we walked a little way up the canyon to the remains of an old stone cabin built by early ranchers and supposedly used by the Wild Bunch. Farther on at Silvertip

Spring, clean water dribbles through a high-walled slot on its way to the roost drainage. Spry Kelsey did some cliff climbing, then showed me the juniper stake corral where it doesn't take much imagination to picture Butch breaking horses.

A shared hostility toward railroad barons and bankers kept the outlaws on good terms with the tough cattlemen who worked this isolated range. Antipathy to outsiders persists among some of them, which is why Kelsey was concerned when we next headed for the Biddlecome-Ekker Ranch at nearby Crow Seep. But I had permission to see the place from Gayemarie Ekker, one of the ranch owners. She then lived in Cedar City, Utah, but she grew up with her mother, Hazel, father, Arthur, and older brother A. C. on the 160-acre Robbers Roost ranch started by her grandfather, Joe Biddlecome, in 1909. The kids learned how to ride and hunted for a robber's stash on nearby Deadman Hill.

"Butch Cassidy was our Robin Hood," Ekker told me.

The snug ranch house and nearby one-room cabin built by Grandpa Joe were deserted when Kelsey and I arrived. They sit on top of the cedar-strewn mesa, with red slickrock in the backyard, the stark profile of the Henry Mountains on the horizon, and a filigree of secret canyons you can't see from above.

Maybe Butch left America in 1901 and never saw home again. Maybe he was just a two-bit crook who didn't look at all like Paul Newman. Maybe everything I found out about him on my trip was a pack of lies. But gazing out over the roost, I knew one thing for sure. The landscape of southern Utah is true blue.

14

RENÉ MAGRITTE'S BRUSSELS

The artist René Magritte spent almost all his life in Brussels. While other surrealists dressed bizarrely, swapped lovers, and made flamboyantly deviant art, he remained an inconspicuous fellow, tending toward portliness, who painted flaming tubas and dismembered body parts every morning in his dining room with the regularity of a bank clerk. His great escape was to put on a bowler hat and walk his dog—a Pomeranian named Loulou—in buttoned-up, bourgeois Brussels.

A story is told about the artist stopping at the corner store to buy some cheese. The grocer started to cut a slice, but Magritte insisted on a piece from another round. When she protested that both were the same, he said, "No, Madame, the one in the window has been looked at all day long by people passing by."

Knowing Belgians, I imagine that madame simply nodded her grizzled head and complied. But visitors to the sane, grey Belgian capital are bound to feel perplexed about how Magritte fit in so comfortably there, indeed, chose it over Paris, where he spent three years from 1927 to 1930 hobnobbing with the wilder French surrealists.

Up until a few years ago, Magritte's steps were hard to trace in Brussels, which made little of him, though by the time of his death in 1967, New York's Museum of Modern Art had mounted a major Magritte retrospective, avant-garde artists such as Andy Warhol and Jasper Johns collected his work, and the Beatles had taken his signature green apple as a logo. Indeed, on my first visit to Brussels in 1994, I had to seek out the room dedicated to him in the Musées Royaux des Beaux Arts.

In 2009, however, the Brussels Beaux Arts literally took Magritte out from under wraps by opening a stand-alone museum dedicated to him in the 18th-century Hotel Altenloh on the Place Royale. For months before the museum opened its doors, the facade was covered by a massive tarp that depicted curtains parting to reveal Magritte's iconic *The Empire of Lights*. By the end of its first year, half a million people had toured the museum, a major new city site that makes it possible to now speak of visiting Magritte's Brussels in the same way people go to Aix-en-Provence for Cézanne and Amsterdam for Van Gogh.

The waiting lines had shortened by the time I visited the Magritte museum recently. Inside its renovated neoclassical façade, I found everything state-of-the-art and 100 percent green (thanks to financial and technical support from the French energy conglomerate GDF Suez), laid out on six levels, with bemusing touches such as bathroom mirrors shaped like Magritte's man in a bowler hat. The galleries follow the artist's development chronologically, beginning with his birth in 1898 and middle-class childhood in the town of Chatelet, about 25 miles south of Brussels.

Anecdotes abound about his youthful peculiarities— playing in cemeteries, celebrating Mass dressed as a priest, hanging yowling cats by their legs on doorbell pull cords— some apparently concocted by Magritte himself. What is known about his childhood is that a hot air balloon once made a crash landing on his rooftop and that his mother drowned herself in the River Sambre when he was 14. But even his contemporary, Freud, would have been hard-pressed to speculate on how these events affected him.

"I detest my past and anyone else's," the artist once said.

Magritte remained adamantly against interpretation, a position curators have tried to respect by portraying the artist through his own pithy words, photos, videos, and other documentary material. "There is no sign of interpretation in the museum," director Michel Draguet has said.

For people like me, who come knowing little more than the

Magritte of bowler hats, the museum offers depth and context. Displays are devoted to his beloved wife, muse, and model Georgette; his bread-and-butter work in advertising; explorations into the relationship between word and image (as in *The Treachery of Images*, his famous 1929 painting of a pipe that is not a pipe, according to the caption); and his break with André Breton and the French surrealists, who appreciated his art but seem to have treated him like a Belgian bumpkin.

Two of the museum's most interesting surprises are artworks from a period of striking stylistic divergence during World War II, when Magritte sought relief from the German Occupation, by painting in the lushly colored manner of Renoir and newly digitalized excerpts from the prankish short movies he made with a Super 8 camera in the late 1950s.

And then there are the masterpieces, beginning with *The Return*, the first Magritte purchased by the museum in 1953, depicting a cutout dove made of cloud-dappled blue sky flying across a nightscape. Bequests by the artist's friends and purchases from the estate of his wife, who died in 1986, enriched the collection, now the largest in the world, including such signature works as *Black Magic* (1945), *The Empire of Lights* (1954), and *The Domain of Arnheim* (1962).

It's an easy walk from the museum down the Mont des Arts, via the elegant Sablon, with its cafes and chocolate shops, to the Royal Academy of Fine Arts on rue du Midi. Enrolled there from 1916 to 1920, Magritte learned how to paint objective reality (so as later to subvert it). But technique interested him almost as little as avant-garde trends such as cubism and futurism. Supported by his father, a businessman, Magritte smoked and drank with friends at the La Fleur en Papier Doré, a cozy, wood-lined café around the corner from the art school.

Then two important things happened: He saw *The Song of Love* by Giorgio de Chirico, which came as a revelation because of the way it made "painting speak of something other than painting," Magritte later said. Afterward, his style began to gel, diverging from surrealism in its accessibility and premeditation, portraying "dreams that are *not* intended to make you sleep but to wake you up," he said.

The second event was running into Georgette Berger while walking in the Brussels Botanic Garden. He knew her from his childhood in Chatelet, but since then, she'd grown into a sizzlingly beautiful young woman. Married in 1922, the couple eventually settled into a flat on rue Esseghem, where they remained until 1954. Before the Hotel Altenloh opened, this small, bare-bones, shotgun apartment in the ordinary, working-class suburb of Jette was the only Magritte museum in Brussels.

A labor of love created by Belgian art collector André Garitte, the museum opened to the public in 1999. Sometimes people turn up there under the mistaken impression that it is the new Musée Royaux Magritte—not such a bad thing, because, with no need for hagiography, rue Essenghem brings to life the man who may have physically inhabited the apartment, but who lived chiefly in his head.

The couple's rez-de-chaussée living quarters have been reassembled so that visitors can see the mantel, staircase, sash window, and keyhole that star in some of Magritte's most famous paintings. At the far end of the back yard, I peeked into the window-lined Studio Dongo, where he did what he called his "idiotic" commercial work.

Many of these rather fetching Art Nouveau cigarette ads, movie posters, and sheet music covers are shown in upstairs galleries, along with special treasures, such as his first juvenile painting of a windmill and some very private erotic art.

The prim villa in the upwardly mobile suburb of Schaerbeek, where Magritte spent his last years, well-off and world famous, is now someone else's house, so there remained just his last resting place to see, though getting there was an exercise in obfuscation. As it turns out, Schaerbeek Cemetery is actually in the town of Evere, near Zaventem Airport. Surrounded by construction, it is no Père Lachaise, and there weren't any signs to help me find his grave.

But a workman gave me directions to the plain marble slab where Magritte lies with Georgette. It bears no panegyrics or plastic flowers, only their names and dates. Pure Magritte. Inconspicuous in death, as in life. The cheese that hasn't been looked at.

❖ ❖

❖ 15 ❖

JULIA'S PARIS

Julia Child wrote bestselling cookbooks, won accolades and awards for her public television cooking shows, made the cover of *Time* magazine, and received the American Medal of Freedom. When she retired, her Cambridge, Massachusetts, kitchen was installed as an exhibit at the Smithsonian Museum of American History in Washington, D.C.

It isn't going too far to say that Child introduced the bland palate of Betty Crocker's America to the transcendent pleasures of French cuisine, thereby broadening the lives and aspirations of many baby boomers, like me, who fricasséed along with her on TV.

That a television cooking teacher could have had such an impact not just on popular culture but on individual Americans was proven by Julie Powell's stupendously successful blog about trying to find herself by making all 524 recipes in Child's 1961 classic, *Mastering the Art of French Cooking*, co-authored with Simone Beck and Louisette Bertholle. The blog became a bestselling book that, together with Child's own 2006 memoir *My Life in France*, inspired the film *Julie and Julia*, written and directed by Nora Ephron.

So what else, I ask, did she have to do to get noticed by the French?

They gave the film *Julie and Julia*, starring Meryl Streep as the ebullient JC, a lackluster reception, even though by the time it was released, America's beloved "French Chef" had been inducted into the French Légion d'Honneur. "In France the ordinary person has no idea who Julia Child is," said her grand-nephew Alex Prud'homme, who helped write her memoir.

I had the pleasure of interviewing JC for the *Los Angeles Times* in 2002. Widowed and pushing 90, she'd moved into a retirement community in Montecito, California, where she still sometimes cooked but had trouble getting around. What I remember most clearly was Julia hefting her long legs into the roomy sport utility vehicle I'd borrowed to take her to lunch at a restaurant in town. "I just love this car," she crooned, sounding like the young Julia again, putting her spoon in a pot de crème.

I was living in Paris when *My Life in France* came out, shortly after she died in 2004, so the book had special meaning for me. As it turned out, the Left Bank apartment she and her husband Paul rented from 1948 to 1953 was right around the corner. Sometimes on my way to the American Library near the Eifel Tower, I'd stop there and think of Julia in the top-floor kitchen, whistling as she put a capon in the oven.

American expats living in Paris have agitated for putting a plaque on the building a few steps away rom the Palais Bourbon. But I'm skeptical that it will ever happen. If the general lack of interest in JC among the French is any indication, it could take a couple of decades for the elegant townhouse where she lived to get an official marker.

Nevertheless, 81 rue de l'Université—Roo de Loo, as the Childs called it—has become something of a place of pilgrimage for American foodies drawn to Paris for an increasing number of cooking programs geared to tourists. Le Cordon Bleu has added an "In Honor of Julia Child" lecture-demonstration to its list of short courses, and Tour de Forks, a New York–based travel company, offers a seven-night "A Taste of Julia Child's Paris and Provence" itinerary.

But you need only a copy of *Appetite for Life*, Noel Riley Fitch's excellent JC biography, or the Child-Prud'homme memoir, *My Life in France*, to follow her in her footsteps—bearing in mind, of course, that it was a different Paris in Julia's time, sans the Musée d'Orsay, the I. M. Pei Pyramid, and the

Pompidou Centre. Les Halles was still a covered food market, and a bistro dinner could be had for $3.

The Childs moved to Paris when Paul got a job working for the US Information Service at the American Embassy. They checked into the Hotel Pont Royal, on the Left Bank just off rue du Bac; breakfasted at the Les Deux Magots, then the haunt of Camus and Sartre; and tried a new restaurant every night. Julia, a gawky 36-year-old from southern California who had never before seen a shallot, had sole meunière three times the first week, but soon ordered more fearlessly and relished everything she tried—escargots, rognons, even tripe.

She and her husband explored Paris from Montmartre to Montparnasse, loving every arrondissement but finally settling down in the Seventh, still favored by expats willing to pay premium prices to live in one of the city's chicest neighborhoods. Pushing my budget to the extreme outer limit, I rented a one-bedroom, fifth-floor walk-up in the heart of the district for $2,800 a month, which I described in my *L.A. Times* "Postcards from Paris" blog. When a number of readers complained that I wasn't getting to know the real, everyday, working-class Paris, I felt chagrinned. Only after reading *My Life in France* did I realize I hadn't moved there for that. I'd moved to Julia's City of Light, circa 1950.

With her, I sauntered along the Quai des Grands-Augustins, read novels in dignified Square Jean XXIII underneath the flying buttresses of Notre Dame, and found all the best little shops tucked along the narrow streets that jig-jag off Boulevard St. Germain: Pain Poilane on the rue du Cherch-Midi, the chocolatier Debauve & Gallais on the rue des Saints-Pères, and Poissonerie du Bac, its iced bins of turbot and cabillaud spilling onto the sidewalk. Around the corner on rue de Grenelle, clerks at Barthélemy, uniformed like milkmaids, advised on the cheese course.

Julia got her produce at Marie des Quattre Saisons on rue de Bourgogne and made friends with the proprietress in Berlitz beginner French. I shopped for fresh fruit and vegetables at Aux Verger de Verneuil, where the redoubtable maitresse studiously ignored me. When she finally threw an extra aubergine in my bag, I felt like popping open a bottle of Veuve Clicquot.

Julia had come to Paris during a period of warmth between France and the United States, stimulated by the Marshall Plan. I arrived about the time President George Bush sent troops into Iraq, a nadir for Franco-American relations. When an *agent de presse* scowled at me for requesting an English-language newspaper, I couldn't help thinking of that ugly old witticism: France is a wonderful country, except for the French.

Then I remembered JC, who thought that the French were the most charming people in the world. The way she took to them without arrogance or inferiority is the endearing heart—and maybe the moral—of her story.

Paul gave her a copy of the *Larousse Gastronomique* for her 37th birthday on August 15, 1949. Two months later, she enrolled at Le Cordon Bleu, now located in the Fifteenth, but near the American Embassy at the time. Under the tutelage of Chef Max Bugnard, she practiced cooking techniques, far more important than learning recipes, she always believed.

Bugnard took the class on a field trip to Les Halles, where Julia became a Saturday morning regular. What a blow it must have been when she learned that the market was demolished in 1971, replaced by the dreary underground mall I found there. But—*quelle joie*—E. Dehillerin, a kitchenware store she adored that is to cooking utensils what Noah's Ark is to the animal kingdom, is still on the north side of the square.

I bought a wire whisk at Dehillerin and tried to bake a soufflé in my toaster oven, one of my rare, generally unsuccessful French cooking efforts. Later I brought a small barbecue back from a visit to the States and set it up on the pocket terrace I could reach only by climbing out the front window of my apartment. There followed several dinner parties à l'Américain featuring baked potatoes and charcoal-grilled steaks, but I gave them up when a guest suggested that barbecuing on the terrace was illegal in Paris.

Mostly I dined out in bistros and cafés, while hankering after the kinds of restaurants Julia frequented. Le Dome, Lapérouse, Le Pharamond, and Chez Jacqueline are still there, but now considerably more touristy and expensive than 50 years ago.

I moved to Rome in 2008—that's a whole other story—but went back to Paris in December 2011 for a visit. A friend and I decided to splurge on dinner at Le Grand Vefour in the Palais Royal. One of the oldest, most sumptuous restaurants in Paris, it was a Julia favorite, where she once spotted an aging Colette in the corner banquette and favored shrimp baked in butter and cream served in a hallowed-out cushion of bread. The Childs had set aside $100 a year for restaurant dinners in Paris. But, even so, Le Grand Vefour must have been a stretch.

My friend sat in Colette's velvet-lined seat, which bears a gold plaque, and tucked into a luscious dish of homard à l'Américain. I had coquilles St. Jacques, prepared à la vapeur, without a trace of the creamy French butter Julia loved. And I can only imagine what she'd have said when the tab came: $700, covering a two-course dinner for both of us and one of the least expensive Sancerres on the *carte des vins*.

Shell-shocked but happy, we chatted with the maître d' who knew JC by reputation. We clearly were not the first Americans to mention her at Le Grand Vefour, though I'd wager many of them don't know who Colette was. Cross-cultural awareness between French and Americans remains "very shallow," Susan Herrmann Loomis, a cooking teacher, author and friend of JC, later reminded me. *Tant pis.*

Still, someday I want to spot a plaque at 81 rue de l'Université that says *Julia Child lived here.*

16

THE CHAIRMAN

Like visitors at George Washington's Mount Vernon estate, people come to Shaoshan village, deep in the heart of China, to remember and teach their children about a national hero.

He launched the Long March, an estimated 3,750-mile epic exploit as central to the story of China as the Boston Tea Party is to America. He fought warlords, the Japanese, and the US-supported Nationalists under Chiang Kai-shek. On October 1, 1949, he stood in Beijing's Tiananmen Square and proclaimed the birth of a new China.

He was Mao Tse-tung.

In the West, he is remembered as the instigator of bloody purges, disastrous agrarian reforms, and that heinous episode of national self-violatiocn known as the Cultural Revolution. The first sentence of *Mao: The Unknown Story*, a unilaterally condemning biography of the Chinese leader published in 2005 by Jung Chang and Jon Halliday, puts it this way: "Mao . . . who for decades held absolute power over the lives of one-quarter of the world's population, was responsible for well over 70 million deaths in peacetime, more than any other 20th century leader."

There is no hint of this at his immaculately preserved birthplace in Shaoshan, the first stop on a trip across China I took to try to resolve in my own mind the apparently irreconcilable contradictions that surround Mao's legacy and modern China. If I were ever to understand why the Communist government acts as it does in matters as consequential as press freedom and

Tibet, it seemed necessary to me, as a foreigner, to try to see China's recent past as the Chinese see it.

Historians and political scientists have been analyzing these questions since Mao died in 1976. But travelers also can study politics and history by visiting places where important—and, in this case, still debated—events occurred that changed the history of China and the world.

The Chinese tourism administration encourages Chinese travelers to visit revolutionary war–era memorials. In 2005, museums opened all along the route of the Long March, which ended in 1935. The arduous trek took the Red Army from compromised Communist strongholds in the south to the dusty town of Yan'an in north-central China. But few foreign visitors add these places to their China itineraries, partly because many of the landmarks are in remote regions. Then too, Westerners seldom know much about China's long, bitter, and—some would claim—ongoing struggle for freedom.

Mao's idyllic-looking childhood home is nestled in a narrow green valley shouldered by rice paddies, a two-hour drive southwest of Changsha, the capital of Hunan province. His modest primary school is close to the entrance of his home, overlooking a pond where I imagined the boy swimming. As were books, swimming was a lifelong passion.

From there, a winding path leads to a tidy, 13-room farm-house where Mao and his two younger brothers worked under the sharp eyes of their father, a comfortably well-off farmer. A steady stream of visitors—mostly old people and students—crowded into the room where Mao, the first surviving son, was born in 1893 on a now-fragile-looking canopy bed to a mother who practiced Buddhism and did housework on bound feet.

One of China's countless heroic statues of the chairman stands at the center of a pavilion outside Shaoshan. Nearby is his clan's peak-roofed ancestral temple, where Mao started a night school for farmers in 1917, an early effort to mobilize China's rural poor, whose hard, hopeless lives were dramatized in Pearl S. Buck's Pulitzer Prize–winning 1931 novel, *The Good Earth*. At a time when the Moscow-educated bosses of the fledgling Chinese Communist Party were trying to get the revolution started in Shanghai, Beijing, and other big cities, Mao understood that real change could come only from the countryside, supported by millions of Chinese peasants.

When I asked my guide what she thought about Mao, she repeated the official assessment rendered by the Communist Party five years after his death. Mao was 30 percent wrong and 70 percent right, a stunning moral quantification now taught to schoolchildren and parroted by the Chinese media.

In Changsha, a burgeoning city with a population in the millions, I caught glimpses of the as-yet-unquantified Mao, an unusually tall youth who loved to eat fermented bean curd, composed poetry, and, according to local lore, mastered the neat trick of reading history books while swimming in the Xiang River. He attended Hunan Fourth Provincial Normal School, a European-style compound devoted to teacher training. There he met and married Yang Kaihui, the daughter of one of his professors. But shortly after Mao led a failed Communist attack on Changsha in 1930, Yang was executed and their three sons were given to relatives.

Mao had four wives and, it's thought, seven children, all subordinated to the revolutionary cause. This pattern, wrote Philip Short in *Mao: A Life*, a massive and balanced biography of the Chinese leader, caused a gradual withering of the man's humanity. Without it, Mao came to believe that China's greatest resource, its people, could be expended to achieve his goals.

A few days later, I traveled by car to one of the most renowned battle sites in the long, gruesome civil war that raged intermittently across China from 1927 to 1950. My guide—a charming young student from Chengdu—told me that all Chinese schoolchildren know what happened at Luding Bridge.

Scholars still contest the events of May 29, 1935, when the hungry, sick, cold, and weary Communists, a little more than halfway through the Long March, made a last-ditch attempt to escape annihilation by the better-armed Nationalists. Early that morning, an advance Red Army unit reached the town of Luding, in a Himalayan mountain valley not far from the Sichuan-Tibet border. There, a 120-yard-long chain-link footbridge spans a deep chasm over the cold, raging Dadu River.

In popular histories and Chinese war movies, a handful of ragged Communist soldiers crawl over the bridge under heavy Nationalist fire from the far bank, blazing the way for the rest of the desperately retreating Red Army. But authors Chang and Halliday claim that there was no battle at the Dadu River, that the Communists crossed the bridge unopposed, and that Mao fabricated the legend of Luding.

A traveler cannot make any final determination about the events, but just getting to the bridge inspires appreciation for the true grit of the Long Marchers. Of the more than 80,000 Red soldiers who began the Long March in 1934, only about 20,000 made it across Luding Bridge in the spring of 1935. I, too, almost didn't make it. I set out with a guide and driver from Chengdu early one spring morning, intending to reach Luding by dark, stopping in the town of Anshunchang, where the Red Army first tried to cross the flooding Dadu. Thwarted, they then embarked on a forced march across about 80 miles of trackless Himalayan foothills to Luding, a feat accomplished in little more than 24 hours. It took me half a day of driving to cover a fraction of that distance, and we never even made it to Anshunchang because the paved road was impassable.

A bridge was out somewhere in that poor, rough, deforested country. Before turning back to the main highway leading to Luding from Chengdu, we passed abandoned hydroelectric plants; burrowed through dark, decrepit tunnels; and saw tired market towns where people still seemed to be suffering from the Great Leap Forward.

While the Cultural Revolution has been officially condemned, attributed to Mao's henchmen in the Gang of Four, the even-more destructive Great Leap is seldom discussed in China. My 20-something guide, a product of the free-market miracle that began after Deng Xiaoping reversed Mao's economic policies in 1978, was too young to remember the famine, but he said his mother and father did. Mao launched the Great Leap in 1958 to jump-start the Chinese economy by turning small peasant farms into collectives, but now it appears to be a major cause of a five-year famine that left at least 30 million people dead.

It was dusk when we finally reached Luding Bridge, where a man in a photography stall with Red Army costumes offered me the chance to have my picture taken dressed up as a Long Marcher. Mao-era kitsch—T-shirts, coffee mugs, alarm clocks bearing the chairman's portrait—has become chic in China, so the photo might have made an amusing souvenir. But the only memory I wanted was of walking over the precarious, swaying footbridge.

At the far side, I asked my guide the same question about Mao that I had asked in Changsha. He repeated the "30 percent bad, 70 percent good" assessment, then added that some Chinese now think 40 percent to 60 percent is a more accurate ratio.

To get to Yan'an several days later, I took a five-hour bus ride north from Xi'an, the capital of Shaanxi Province, on a new superhighway that ascends the Yellow Earth Plateau. The monotonous, inhospitable landscape, where people live in cave houses built into the sides of canyons, is riven by erosion and subject to Old Testament–force dust storms. But the Communists found safe haven in Yan'an for more than a decade, from shortly after the end of the Long March through the expulsion of Japanese forces from China in 1945 and the Communist Party's final battles against Chiang Kai-shek. In this small town in the Chinese hinterlands, Mao consolidated his position as supreme leader and developed the ideologies canonized in his *Little Red Book.*

My guide in Yan'an was a pleasant, soft-spoken man who took me through the Communists' compound at Yangjialing, near the mouth of a dry valley just north of town. By late afternoon, the compound was crowded with uniformed groups of Communist Party members and Chinese soldiers on holiday, all snapping pictures of the assembly hall where Mao delivered his infamously long speeches and the cave apartment where he lived.

Tunneled into the hillside, the chairman's quarters have the pleasantly musty smell of a wine cellar and a feeling of security that must have appealed to Long March veterans.

From the canopy bed, which is theatrically littered with

cigarette butts, Mao directed the wars against the Japanese and the Nationalists. It was also the perch from which he wrote, read, and devised the Yan'an Rectification campaign, aimed at purifying the beliefs of new recruits to the Communist Party and ensuring that they recognized Mao as its final authority. The campaign was a precursor of the ugly purges to follow.

Visitors can experience how the party leaders lived during that time at the Yangjialing Cave Hotel, up the canyon from the compound. Its rooms sit on half a dozen levels on the hill, with a restaurant below and a tea garden on top. My room had a platform bed, where I felt safe and grounded during a thunderstorm that rocked the little valley.

The night I arrived, so did a bus carrying 150 new party recruits on a visit from Beijing, where they worked for a high-tech company. They looked to be in their 20s and 30s, and, clad in orange polo shirts, they paraded around the courtyard behind a flag bearer. Afterward, they listened to a lecture by a local historian and watched old Chinese revolutionary war movies alfresco. It looked about as diabolical as an Amway convention.

Later, my guide said that only about 5 percent of the Chinese people belong to the party, partly because of the many rules members must follow. Cynicism and apathy are other factors, increasing since China's economic opening and the 1989 killing of pro-democracy demonstrators in Beijing's Tiananmen Square

That's where I ended my tour, gazing at the iconic portrait of Mao on the Gate of Heavenly Peace. The chairman's image has presided over the vast square since 1949, though it had to be replaced a few years ago after an unemployed man tried to set it on fire. Crowds stood below the portrait, some from abroad, but most of them Chinese who now have enough money and the freedom to travel, something I have always taken for granted. The horrors of the 20th century—the crushing poverty and hopelessness, the wars and revolutions, the natural and man-made disasters—are behind them now, and the picture of Mao is more a symbol of China than the image of a real man who lived on a gargantuan scale. Some Westerners think the evils

Mao perpetuated blot out whatever real reforms he brought to China, a conclusion the Chinese may someday reach, too. Meanwhile, I can only begin to imagine what it will mean to them to have to decide whether their nation's founder was a George Washington or a Joseph Stalin.

Looking up at the chairman's portrait in Tiananmen Square, I remembered the words of a friend who says sanity lies in the ability to live with contradictions. At Yan'an, Shaoshan, and Luding Bridge, that was all I could do.

17

OF SWORD FIGHTS AND STOLEN KISSES

Standing in the rain atop Carlton Hill, I could see the icy blue Firth of Forth. When the wind tried to grab my coat, I spun around and found the tapestry of Edinburgh at my feet, built up solidly between city and bay. But when I looked through my mind's eye, I could see the capital of the wild, green kingdom that 17-year-old Mary Stuart inherited from her father, King James V of Scotland.

Everyone who comes here, it seems, knows about the hapless Scottish queen whose execution for treason in 1587 at the behest of her cousin, Elizabeth I of England, has inspired books, plays, movies, and continuing debate. When Elizabeth died childless in 1603, Mary's son, James VI of Scotland, was summoned to the English throne, uniting two incessantly warring realms into the nation we now know as Great Britain.

Once upon a time, I read every book about Mary in the library, most of them fictionalized accounts of her life that filled in the blanks left by history with sword fights and stolen kisses. To me, she was a brave and beautiful 16th-century Princess Diana, ruled by her heart, ensnarled in events she couldn't control.

Historians have been equally fascinated by Mary, though their assessments have varied dramatically over time. In the immediate aftermath of her death, fellow Catholics thought of her as a martyr, while tracts appeared in Protestant Scotland that called her a traitor and libertine. More recent considerations, including Antonia Fraser's 1969 biography, have sought to balance the quotients of scoundrel and saint, without finally determining what kind of woman she was. So I came to Scotland trusting in travel to resolve the mystery or, at least, to help me remember why she once starred in my dreams.

By the time Mary landed at Leith just north of Edinburgh in 1561, she had been through more sorrows and joys than most people know in a lifetime. Her father, James V, died just days after she was born, lamenting that he had not been able to give the kingdom a male heir. Crowned queen of Scotland as a babe-in-arms, she had enough royal blood to sit on the throne of England as well (were Henry VIII not already occupying it). She was stalked by English armies and then taken to France for safekeeping; she eventually married Francis, the dauphin, who ascended the French throne a year later. Together, they ruled France for 13 months before he died of an ear infection in 1560, leaving Mary a young widow with one crown left—but one she had to return to Scotland to claim.

That is why I started my pilgrimage looking toward Leith, wondering how Mary, reared in the cultivated French court, felt when she set foot in Scotland. By all accounts, it was a cold, wet, poor, perpetually war-torn country on the fringe of European civilization, governed in her absence by a group of lords who, unlike devoutly Catholic Mary, had embraced the Protestant Reformation. According to Brantome, a French courtier who accompanied Mary to Scotland, the horses provided to take her party from Leith to the Palace of Holyroodhouse were pitiful nags compared with the steeds she had ridden in France. Mary was an accomplished equestrian, statuesque, her mantle flying behind her. She spoke perfect French but hadn't forgotten the language of her people, which endeared her to commoners who lined the roads hoping for a glimpse of the goddess. On landing, she immediately would have spied dour, gray Edinburgh Castle, but the royal party headed instead to Holyroodhouse on the eastern side of town, beneath the volcanic crag known as Arthur's Seat. Built around a medieval abbey, Holyroodhouse was Scotland's finest royal residence, turreted and towered in the manner of a Loire Valley chateau.

Today, the graceful palace faces the Scottish Parliament, a contemporary nightmare of a building opened in 2004. I pretended it wasn't there, went to the palace gate, and bought a ticket, which includes an audio guide. The forecourt was the first stop, where, the guide said, Queen Elizabeth II approved the 1998 act that gave Scotland home rule for the first time in almost 300 years.

Sovereignty was also the question when Mary first saw Holyroodhouse Palace. In the political chess game played by France and England, Scotland, and, more specifically Mary, were the prizes. When the Scots annulled a treaty betrothing her to Henry VIII's son, Edward, the English king sent troops across the border into battles known as the Rough Wooing. Her marriage to the French dauphin made the English apoplectic, and she was an incessant nettle in the flesh of Henry's daughter by Anne Boleyn, Elizabeth I, whom Catholics considered an illegitimately born usurper to the throne.

Mary settled into apartments in the northwestern tower at Holyroodhouse, the backdrop for many of the most dramatic events in her life. Shortly after she arrived, she sparred over theology with John Knox in her audience chamber. The Protestant Moses of 16th-century Scotland and founder of the Presbyterian faith, he was a virulent misogynist who likened Mary to Nero. But after their meeting, he gave the young queen a left-handed compliment: "If there be not in her a proud mind, a crafty wit and an indurate heart against God and His truth, my judgment faileth me."

Knox's house is just down the Royal Mile from Holyroodhouse, as is his church, St. Giles' Cathedral, where he still stands in sculpted stone ranting against "the monstrous regiment of women."

Mary didn't disappoint him, though she got off to a promising start in Scotland by laboring to reconcile her incessantly feuding nobles and vowing to respect the Protestant status quo as long as she could practice her Catholic faith in private. But four years after she arrived, she made the first of many missteps by marrying her handsome cousin Henry Stuart, Lord Darnley, in the now-ruined Holyroodhouse chapel. Mary, it seems, had fallen in love and meant to indulge her passion.

But her choice was disastrous. By all accounts, Darnley was a wastrel who drank to excess, contracted syphilis, and plotted the slaying of Mary's secretary, Italian musician David Rizzio on March 9, 1566. Mary and a few attendants, including Rizzio, were dining in a small room adjoining her bedchamber at Holyroodhouse when Darnley burst in, followed by a clutch of armed noblemen who tore Rizzio from Mary's arms. Pregnant at the time, she watched in horror as they stabbed him repeatedly. The chamber where Rizzio died is now a gallery with such treasures as a small French portrait of Mary from 1559 and a sample of the Scottish queen's baby-fine needlework.

For a sheer historical jolt, nothing tops Holyroodhouse, though the National Museum of Scotland on Chambers Street has a copy of the marble sarcophagus beneath which she was buried in London's Westminster Abbey.

The atmospheric ruins of Linlithgow Palace, Mary's birthplace, and Stirling Castle, where the infant queen was crowned in 1543, are an easy drive west of the capital. A small museum is devoted to Mary in the market town of Jedburgh, about 50 miles southeast of the Scottish capital, and pilgrims can find no better place for a picnic than Lochleven Castle on an island in a lake about 25 miles north of Edinburgh, where rebel lords imprisoned her in 1567.

But tucked in some of her erstwhile kingdom's most beguiling corners are other less touristy Queen of Scots sites, most of them stately homes she visited, including Traquair House in the Tweed River Valley, about an hour's drive south of Edinburgh. The white, gabled house with a row of chimneys on its steeply pitched roof dates from the twelfth century and has been in the same Scottish Catholic noble family since 1491. When I visited, Catherine Maxwell Stuart, the 21st Lady of Traquair, was living there with her family, except in the high season, when she makes the house available to bed-and-breakfast guests.

I got the lovely Rose Room on the second floor overlooking a maze. Just down the hall is the chamber where Mary stayed in 1566, furnished with family heirlooms including the cradle used for the queen's new baby, James, born shortly after Rizzio's death. Overnight guests can wander through the museum, libraries, chapel, and salons as if they were their own.

It's hard to think of unpleasantness at lovely Traquair House, but at the time of their visit, Mary and Darnley were hopelessly alienated because of the role he had played in Rizzio's killing, though she tried to keep up a felicitous front. One day, she excused herself from the hunt on the pretext that she might be pregnant again. Drunk as usual, Darnley protested, "Ought we not work a mare well when she is in foal?"

At Traquair House, I wandered along sodden paths by the Tweed, hoping Mary had found consolation in the green meadows and gorse-covered moors that enfold the valley. I also elicited opinions from Lady Maxwell Stuart, whose sympathy lies solidly with the queen, and from Ronald Morrison, a member of the Marie Stuart Society, a group of British history devotees.

"It's fair to say that Mary was wronged, but she made mistakes," he told me over lunch at the Traquair House cafe. Among them, he cited her choice of husbands, her pretensions to the English crown, and whatever role she may have played in Darnley's demise, less than a year after Rizzio, at Kirk o' Field house in Edinburgh, where he was recovering from syphilis while the queen was lodged at Holyroodhouse. Historians agree that a group of plotters, led by swashbuckling James Hepburn, fourth Earl of Bothwell, set off an explosion at Kirk o' Field intended to rid Scotland of Darnley, though his body was found in the garden. He had been strangled.

The rest of the facts are murky. Did Mary know of the plot or even participate in it? By that time had she fallen in love with Bothwell, whom she wed three months later. Or did the ambitious earl rape and strong-arm her into marriage, as some historians claim?

Even now, I hate to think the worst of Mary. The romantic in me wants to believe that she and Bothwell were true lovers, fighting for their lives against the Scottish lords who rallied against them. With a rebel army at their heels, they fled to

Borthwick Castle, on a hill overlooking the River Esk about 15 miles south of Edinburgh.

Owned by an ally of Bothwell, stout, twin-towered Borthwick Castle, built in 1430, is now a hotel with 10 baronial chambers linked by spiral staircases hard enough to climb in my old sneakers, let alone in Mary's heavy skirts and dainty satin heels.

I had dinner next to a set of armor in the castle's vaulted Great Hall, finished with a tot of single malt Scotch from one of the bottles lining the window through which, dressed as a boy, Mary escaped besieging rebels. From there she rode through Curry Woods to nearby Crichton Castle, now an evocative ruin where sparrows nest, into battle with insurgents, and, when that was lost, across the border to England, where she hoped for help from her cousin Elizabeth.

Mary never again saw Bothwell, who fled to Denmark. She spent the next 18 years and 9 months a captive in England, where some say that she was framed for treason by William Cecil, Queen Elizabeth's trusted secretary of state. Elizabeth signed Mary's 1587 death warrant, the queen's hands tied by law even though she may have wanted to spare Mary—another question left hanging.

After dinner, I retired to my room, which is where the queen stayed 400 years earlier. For a Mary fan, there could be no greater bliss than watching darkness steal into the slit-windowed nooks beneath the gables and reading in the massive red-canopied bed. I had Fraser's excellent biography in hand, but I dreamed that night of the beautiful, passionate, and tragic queen I'd loved as a girl.

❖ 18 ❖

HAPPY ENDINGS ON THE FAIRY TALE ROAD

Clever Elsie, my favorite Grimms' fairy tale, is about a silly, slothful woman who won't change her ways. Her husband, Hans, catches her asleep near the field where he has sent her to work, so he throws a net woven with little bells over her head, goes home, and locks the door. When she wakes up in the dark, she feels confused about where and who she is, and the bells don't help. Jingling, she goes home, raps on the window, and asks if Elsie's there.

"Yes," Hans answers, "she is at home."

"Oh, dear," she cries, "then I am not Clever Elsie after all," and runs away, never to be heard of again.

My mother read this story to me when I was a child, and I loved it, because Elsie made me laugh. As time went on, I kept her in my heart, the way many people do with a fairy tale hero or heroine. She reminds me of my past, although the story scares me a little because she slipped so easily into the dark world of craziness.

Wilhelm Grimm, the younger of the two German brothers who collected and popularized stories like *Clever Elsie*, wrote that fairy tales are full of "fragments of belief dating back to most ancient times, in which spiritual things are expressed in a figurative manner."

Folklorists and psychologists have devoted careers to picking apart the stories that the Grimms collected, trying to decipher their meaning and determine whether some of them—such as *The Pied Piper of Hamelin*, about a town that loses all its children—may be based in fact.

That's partly why I went to the region of north-central Germany, where the Grimms lived and collected their tales, searching for the settings of stories like *Clever Elsie*. There would be ducks and geese in the yards she passed by, cobbled lanes leading to an old church, shops with strings of sausage and pumpernickel bread, farm fields bordered by forests, and, in the distance, a castle on a hill exactly like those in the pictures that adorned my childhood storybooks.

The German Fairy Tale Road, or Marchenstrasse, runs for 400 miles from Frankfurt to Bremen (where, in *The Town Musicians*, another Grimm story, a band of broken-down farm animals seeks their fortune). I covered the southern part of the tour from Frankfurt to Hanover, which promised the greatest concentration of fairy tale sites: hamlets with medieval half-timbered houses slumbering in the soft folds of valleys, drained by beautiful rivers like the Weser and surrounded by carefully managed forests like Reinhardswald, where Sleeping Beauty is said to have dozed for a hundred years.

Of course, no one knows for sure where these stories really took place, because most are based on orally transmitted tales that predate dawn-of-history migrations into the area of central Europe that is now Germany. Scholarly Jacob and Wilhelm Grimm traced some of the stories in their landmark *Nursery and Household Tales,* published in 1812, to Charles Perrault's 17th-century *Tales of Mother Goose*, which, in turn, is thought to have tapped sources such as the *Arabian Nights*, dating from tenth-century India and Persia. But this hasn't stopped tourist offices in towns along the Marchenstrasse from claiming Little Red Riding Hood and Snow White as their own.

I don't recommend this trip for little ones, because, apart from summertime puppet theaters and the occasional "leisure" and "aqua" parks, there are no Disney-esque magic castles along the way. This is a trip for adults in search of their inner children, with lots of patience and a good sense of direction, although even they are apt to get lost. I erred countless times on back roads that didn't seem to correspond to the markings on my map. I bought more detailed maps and got lost again.

Between the towns of Alsfeld and Kassel, about halfway through my drive, I found myself in the village of Sondheim, which reminded me of the theme song from Stephen Sondheim's 1987 musical about fairy tales, *Into the Woods*. It has such lyrics as, "Into the woods, and down the dell; the path is straight, I know it well." Humming it helped stem my aggravation, and gradually I came to understand that getting lost was an important part of the program, just as it was for the characters in the Grimms' tales and the Sondheim musical. You have to get lost in the woods to find out anything about who you are and the road you should take through life, both seem to say. Better still to be led there by a fairy tale character like Elsie, who, crazy though she was, I can't help but follow. I started in Hanau, 10 miles east of Frankfurt, where Jacob and Wilhelm Grimm were born in 1785 and 1786, respectively, to the fiercely patriotic town clerk and lawyer Philipp Wilhelm Grimm and his wife, Dorothea. Hanau is now more a modern city suburb than the prim town it must have been in the late 18th century, when Napoleon was building an army in France that would soon overrun Europe, including the Grimms' little home duchy of Hesse-Cassel.

Hanau has a wide-open marketplace bordered by an 18th-century town hall, shops and cafes, where I had my first bratwurst and beer of the trip and gazed at my first statue of the Brothers Grimm: Jacob, seated with a book in his hands, and Wilhelm, reading over his sibling's shoulder. The bronze captures the spirit of loving brotherhood and collaboration that, by all accounts, lasted throughout their lives, culminating not just in their beloved collection of fairy tales but also in groundbreaking scholarly works on the German language and mythology, produced, for the most part, in a shared study with a desk for each Grimm. Murray B. Peppard, author of *Paths Through the Forest: A Biography of the Brothers Grimm*, portrays Jacob as a hair-splitting academic and crotchety bachelor, called "the old man" by his university students even when he was relatively young. His sternness and diligence were due partly to the death of their father in 1796, when the boys were not yet teenagers. Wilhelm had a milder, more charming nature; he married and had a family, with whom elder brother Jacob sometimes lived.

For easy touring of the area around Steinau, where the Grimm family lived from 1791 to 1798 and where there is a museum devoted to them, I stayed for two nights at a family-run hotel with a half-timbered facade, brown woodwork balconies, and overflowing flower boxes in the town of Gelnhausen, just off the A66 autobahn, about 12 miles northeast of Hanau. The Hotel Burg-Muhle, which occupies the site of a 13th-century mill, has an inviting restaurant, where I had a dinner of pork loin with creamy Dauphine potatoes. The guest rooms were tidy and comfortable, with, alas, little character, like so many others in which I stayed on this trip.

But one morning, after a night of hard rain, the receptionist said in English, "The sun is coming out, as it should," which somehow sounded perfectly German. And I liked the hotel's location, near the ox-bowing Kinzig River and the ruddy red, late Gothic and Romanesque ruins of the palace of Frederick I.

Known as Barbarossa, or Redbeard, Frederick I (1123–1190) is thought to have inspired some of the Grimms' villainous kings, such as the one in *Many-Fur* who loses his beautiful wife and decides that his daughter is the only woman who can replace her. Covered by a coat of animal skins, she flees but reappears to dance in disguise with the king at a ball in a palace that must have looked like Barbarossa's. As the last note of music dies, she vanishes, but he soon finds and claims her as his second wife.

Sex, violence, incest, and infanticide aren't uncommon in the Grimms' collection, which was meant, at least initially, more as a cultural repository than as entertainment for children. In ensuing editions—seven in all during the Grimms' lifetimes—some troubling material was toned down, leaving most of the tales with happy endings or moral lessons (like Elsie's not-very-convincing "So, after all, it is better to be industrious than clever").

But psychologist Bruno Bettelheim says in his 1976 study of

fairy tales, *The Uses of Enchantment*, that children can tolerate the stories' moral ambiguity, sex, and violence because it helps them find meaning in life. "The fairy tale," he says, "takes these existential anxieties and dilemmas very seriously and addresses itself directly to them: the need to be loved and the fear that one is thought worthless; the love of life, and the fear of death." (After Bettelheim's suicide in 1990, his research methods and ethics came under fire, but *The Uses of Enchantment* still stands as a landmark in fairy tale interpretation.)

A short walk from the palace ruins is further reason for existential anxiety and a reminder that even some of the most outlandish elements in the Grimms' stories have real under-pinnings: a tower where, in the 16th century, witches were kept before being burned at the stake or drowned in the river. Atop the hill in the center of Gelnhausen is St. Mary's Lutheran Church, built in the twelfth century, with interior carvings of fire-breathing serpents and horned monsters that may as well be illustrations of the Grimms' tales.

At a butcher shop on a steeply pitched lane, where there were sausages of all shapes and sizes—marbled, mottled, and checker boarded—a clerk helped me choose a tasty-but-not-too-adventurous ham and cheese sandwich on which I picnicked in the square.

The next day, I got lost driving from Gelnhausen to Steinau on a circuitous route through thick stands of pine that made me think of Hansel and Gretel and their father, a poor wood-cutter who lets their stepmother persuade him to abandon the children in the forest. Steinau, the Grimms' childhood home, turned out to be a pretty German hamlet, with half-timbered shop fronts leading to a square and a pentagonal castle, built by 16th-century counts of Hanau. When I finally got to Steinau, I felt as though I'd found my way to a happy ending.

No one spoke English at the Brothers Grimm house and museum, in another half-timbered edifice, with a courthouse on the first floor and magistrate's quarters on the second. And the displays were captioned only in German. So I had to intuit my way through them, noting little brother Ludwig Emil Grimm's illustrations of the fairy tales, the re-creation of an

18th-century Hessian kitchen, and intricate needlework done by Charlotte, the brothers' only sister. I found a carving of the Frog Prince on the fountain in the Steinau square and toured the castle, where the docent's towheaded son ran through in a paper wimple like the ones Cinderella's wicked stepsisters wore. The town's fairy tale puppet theater was dark, so I ended my day with a dinner of salty potato soup and chicken in a thick, hearty Riesling sauce at the cozy Hotel-Restaurant-Cafe Burgmann-enahus, built in 1589.

Then it was on to Lauterbach, a thriving market town with two castles and a historic downtown, where I heard an organist practicing a fugue in the stately Baroque church and bought a slice of apple strudel at a bakery. Lauterbach is associated with *Snow White and the Seven Dwarfs* in tourist brochures, largely because it's where plastic garden gnomes are manufactured. I wanted one for my kitsch collection, and went from one store to another, where there were planters and hoses but no gnomes. One clerk told me smugly that they'd gone out of style.

You'll find the half-timbered houses of the German Middle Ages, with their steeply canted eaves, lace-curtained windows, and stout, crisscrossing wood beams, all along the Marchen-strasse. Alsfeld, about 10 miles north of Lauterbach on Route 254, where I stopped for lunch, has some of the finest examples of half-timbering in the country, including its twin-towered Old Town Hall, built in 1512.

Then I headed for the city of Kassel, where the Brothers Grimm went to high school in 1798, served as librarians for the King of Westphalia, and edited the first volumes of *Nursery and Household Tales* before accepting positions at the University of Göttingen.

I still had a whole afternoon ahead of me for getting lost on the way to Kassel, first around the villages of Treysa and Schwalm-stadt, on the Schwalm River. The area has a right to claim Little Red Riding Hood as its own by virtue of the red caps local women wear on festival days. Moreover, Dorothea Viehmann, the peasant woman who told the Grimms many of the tales that ended up in their collection, lived in this bucolic, rolling region. But I couldn't find Granny's house or a red cap anywhere.

Then I had an epiphany: I wasn't going to find Granny's house, because it exists only in the imagination. So I needed to be less slavish in my pursuit of fairy tale settings and wander aimlessly, like Hansel and Gretel. On a whim, I turned off the main road and found Sondheim, followed by pretty Neukirchen and Oberaula, all picture-postcard-perfect villages, surmounted by a medieval town hall and church, ringed by farm fields and forests, light and dark, sunshine and shade. I was fairly sure that this was where Elsie ran from house to house.

The countryside wasn't spectacular, like the Austrian Alps, but I realized that the credibility of the tales benefits from the pleasing, cozy German landscapes where the Grimms set them. Perhaps we can feel the fear conjured by fairy tale witches and giants only when they spring from such comfortable, workaday places.

I reached Kassel after dark. The city where the Grimms lived in the early part of the 19th century is now sprawling and modern; most of its historic sections were leveled during World War II. But I found a place to stay—the little Hotel Garni Ko 78, with a cheerful single overlooking a garden. At breakfast, I met a man from Frankfurt who told me that his mother wouldn't read him the Grimms' tales when he was a boy. This is hardly surprising. Just after the war, Allied occupying forces banned *Nursery and Household Tales* in several German cities because the collection was thought to reflect the nation's proclivity for cruelty and violence.

The Museum of the Brothers Grimm is in a dignified, lemon-yellow mansion built in 1714 that overlooks the wide Baroque park at the center of Kassel. It has family mementos, including Wilhelm's 1804 report card, neatly penned letters Jacob wrote to his family when he was a university student in nearby Marburg, a drawing of storyteller Dorothea Viehmann, and a whole floor of displays on how the tales were illustrated over the years.

Beyond the museum, little remains of the Grimms in Kassel. But I was glad I spent part of the day at Schloss Wilhemshohe, a magnificent 18th-century royal palace museum just west of town, surrounded by cafes, gardens, lakes, fountains, and architectural curios such as an ersatz medieval castle, forests with well-maintained paths, and sweeping lawns where lovers picnic and children tussle.

Soon, though, I had to move on, because my goal that night was about 50 miles north of Kassel, in the hamlet of Sababurg, ringed by a game park and the ancient forest of Reinhardswald. The road there led past lovely Munden, with its 650-year-old bridge, and along the west bank of the graceful Weser River. As I approached Sababurg and caught sight of its castle-hotel nestled in the treetops, I gave in to fairy tale fantasizing, knowing that I'd rest that night in a turret room like the one where the Sleeping Beauty of my childhood slumbered. For me, she isn't the talisman that Clever Elsie is, but like many women, I suspect, I've always harbored a hope that I'd someday be awakened by the kiss of a handsome prince.

I got no such kiss, but I wasn't disappointed. With its twin-steepled towers and old vine-laced stone walls, the castle-hotel captures the spirit of the Sleeping Beauty tale and seems to be waiting for the narcoleptic spell to break. It was originally built in 1334, then fell to ruin, was rebuilt as a hunting lodge in 1522, and opened as an elegant country inn in 1960. Inside is a restaurant that specializes in such dishes as venison soup, guinea fowl, and plum tart with cinnamon sauce. After dinner, to reach my room, I had to walk up a flight of stone steps, down a carpeted hall, and around a spiral staircase decorated with hunting prints and an antique spinning wheel. My room was small but pretty, with matching yellow curtains and bedspread and a bay window through which I watched the sun set over the fairy-tale forest.

It was raining when I woke the next morning, but that didn't stop me from taking a walk around the game park, where I heard boars grunting in a pen and the sound of chain saws in the distance. On the drive out of the woods to Route 83, which would lead me eventually to the handsome spa town of Bad Karlshafen, Hameln, and, finally, Hanover, I stopped in Trendelburg, which has a castle with a tower like the one in which Rapunzel was locked. In the earliest Grimm version of the story, it's fairly clear that the prince who visited her by climbing her tresses got her pregnant. ("Tell me, Godmother," Rapunzel says to the witch after repeated trysts with the prince, "why my clothes are so tight and why they don't fit me any longer.")

Bettelheim found intimations of sex in the kisses of handsome princes and evidence of first menses in needle pricks. But he says nothing about the mysterious flute-playing kidnapper in *The Pied Piper of Hamelin*, from the Grimms' *German Legends*. This is probably because *The Pied Piper* is more a folk tale than a fairy story, rooted in history and place. In an ancient manuscript that dates the tale to 1284, a man with a pipe was said to have lured away 130 children.

Now spelled "Hameln," the town has an astonishing collection of elaborately decorated half-timbered structures, including the Hotel zur Krone, where I stayed for a night, and its neighbor, the early 17th-century "Rat Catcher's House," which got its name because of an inscription in its stone facade identifying the alleyway beside it as the route through which the children were abducted.

The town has hardly forgotten the Pied Piper. Shops along the main street sell rat-catcher key chains and pastries. In the summer, actors perform the Pied Piper story on the square, and several times a day, all year long, a mechanical piper emerges on the west facade of the town office building, a Renaissance whirligig known as the "Wedding House," to lure away the town's kids.

Scholars have suggested that Hameln's little ones may have been wooed away by an agent of the Count of Schaumburg, seeking colonists for new territories in Moravia; that they were the underage knights and pilgrims of one of the Children's Crusades of the Middle Ages; and that they were victims of a St. Vitus' Dance plague that made its sufferers shake so hard it looked as though they were dancing. The tale has it that they were spirited away because the town failed to pay the piper for exterminating its rats. The lesson of the story is clear: What would the world be like without children?

And what would it be like without fairy tales, which continue to resist easy analysis and, as I discovered, are hard to pin to a place?

Driving the Marchenstrasse was frustrating, because I

expected to find places that don't exist. Still, it was right for me to go into the woods, where I came to understand that, no matter how much I identify with Elsie, I don't have to meet the same fate. I will never run from house to house looking for myself, because I know who I am, even if I sometimes get lost.

"This is exactly the message that fairy tales get across," Bettelheim wrote, "that a struggle against severe difficulties in life is unavoidable, is an intrinsic part of the human experience—but if one steadfastly meets unexpected and often unjust hardships, one masters all obstacles and at the end emerges victorious."

PART 3
SOUVENIRS

Memories are scattered all over the world. We must travel to find them.

I don't remember where I read that, or whether my paraphrasing is entirely accurate. I know only that it is so, that we rediscover things about ourselves that we've forgotten—or perhaps never fully appreciated—by moving widely and freely around the world. On a bench at the Forbidden City, I think of my brother and call him. In Edinburgh, chasing Mary, Queen of Scots, I meet my romantic 16-year-old self. On the island of Lipari, I understand why my Italian grandfather came to the States.

By and large, journalists write impersonally; they write about facts. But the travel writer who follows suit misses the best stuff, what comes of a personal encounter with place and its novelties, the deep interior monologue that unfolds while driving over the American Great Plains or taking an endless train ride across China. Think Bruce Chatwin, Robert Louis Stevenson, Martha Gellhorn.

The pieces that follow reflect the times I've been able to speak in the first person singular—to write about the memories I've found in, among other places, County Clare, Ireland, and Trader Joe's in Los Angeles.

❖ 19 ❖

MY MOTHER'S BOOTS

The first travel story I wrote for the *New York Times* was about a week I spent walking the chalk downs of Wiltshire, a county about 75 miles west of London. It was May, and the paths I tramped were sloppy. But I was prepared, because I'd packed a pair of 30-year-old boots my mother had produced from the bottom of a closet before I left and bestowed on me, her youngest daughter.

Those boots served me well in England, led me past ruins of Iron Age forts, took me up the mossy steps of medieval churches; they finally came home encrusted with gray Wiltshire clay.

I had no reason to summon my mother's boots to duty again until a year or so later, when I was assembling gear for a Kentucky spelunking adventure. At the time, I was just starting to really travel, which is why that trip became an exercise in taking risks and testing my limits. On it I did a lot of things I probably shouldn't have, like climbing into caves without a flashlight and hiking alone on trails known to be sunbathing spots for poisonous snakes. I always liked to get a rise out of my mother, so when I got home, I told her about my adventures. She was a worrywart for as long as I knew her, but she just smiled and said that a person can strike out in boots like hers without fear of snakebite.

After many excursions in my mother's boots, I've begun to suspect that they are magic. I never wear them without seeing

131

inspiring sights, experiencing life and nature more deeply, and coming home changed. I can rarely say how, but more and more this is the reason I travel.

My mother's boots are chestnut tan, Boy Scout standard issue, purchased about the time she bought a virtually identical pair for my brother, while suiting him up to win a chest full of merit badges. They are lined with wrinkles now, familiar to a certain Italian shoe repairman in the West Village of New York, who told me to throw them away two springs ago before I went for a hike along the Brittany coast. But I insisted that he sew the tongues back in, flew to France, and set off, at first barefoot in the sand north of St. Malo and then trustingly shod all the way to Mont St. Michel. I *do* know how that walk changed me. I realized that there is no good reason to be cynical when you're eating oysters in Cancale and lying in clover above the Atlantic Ocean at the Pointe de la Varde. The world is beautiful, if you have boots to see it with.

Back home, I called my mother and told her so. But she wanted to know something more mundane. "Are the bindings of the boots coming out? The bindings were coming out the year I didn't climb Longs."

For nearly 10 summers during my childhood, my family spent two weeks at a YMCA camp just outside the Rocky Mountains National Park in Colorado. My mother broke in her boots while hiking over the Front Range. Whenever I lace my mother's boots up, that place comes back to me, especially 14,256-foot Longs Peak, the patriarch of the Front Range.

"Why didn't you make Longs?" I prodded. "Dad and Johnnie did."

"Because of you," she said, and then I recalled the trial and tribulation I was to her when she took me for a climb. I remember crying all the way up Deer Mountain—puny by anyone's estimation, except mine, at ten.

My mother loved the mountains and cut a dashing figure among them, a red bandanna around her neck, her hair blowing free—so unlike the woman who, back home, cooked dinners, ironed, and spent every Saturday morning at the beauty parlor. When she tried to leave me at the Y's children's program, I cried and screamed, in effect holding her hostage while my father and brother conquered Longs.

We talked about this, she without rancor. "I'd rather be a mother than a mountain climber," she says. But then, "I know I could have made Longs."

Indeed, she could have. She went to places I may never see, sunk her feet in the sand around the pyramids, touched Alaskan glaciers. A social studies teacher, she saw travel as a way of learning. Because of her, my vacations are never vacant. Places mean something, and it's up to me to find out what it is—that was my mother's legacy.

But as a symbol, they're complex. When I climb mountains in them, I feel as if, by rights, my mother should be there. I never could imagine making the kinds of sacrifices she made for her children, which is partly why I never had any. And she never pushed me.

I've wondered, though, what I'm missing. Could it be that life is really more about making sacrifices than reaching mountain summits? Is this what I'm to take from my mom—a woman who in all respects was, in my eyes, successful? Then why did she give me her boots, if not to urge me to climb on?

"We think back through our mothers if we are women," Virginia Woolf wrote.

On my 40th birthday, I climbed Longs, in my mother's boots, of course. A fellow hiker recorded my ascent with a camera, mostly for the benefit of my doubtful father and brother. When I got the pictures back, I stood in the camera shop amazed, because in the picture of me at the top, I look so oddly like my mother. Oddly, because I'm the image of my dad. But on the top of Longs, I looked like her.

My mother's boots are one legacy I guess I won't pass on. Maybe they are more a link than a legacy, between mother and daughter, two travelers on the same journey.

❖ ❖

❖ 20 ❖

HOW DO I SAY "I'M LOST"?

A Chinese proverb perfectly sums up the months I spent studying Mandarin in Beijing: To suffer and learn, one pays a high price, but a fool can't learn any other way.

The infamously difficult Chinese language could make a fool out of anyone. Standard Chinese, known as Mandarin or *putonghua*, has tens of thousands of characters, many taking more than 20 strokes to write, and a transliteration system called pinyin that expresses Chinese words in the 26 letter Latin alphabet of English. The grammar seems deceptively simple. But consider such anomalies as noun classifiers known as "measure words" and rules of sentence construction that put objects before verbs. To make matters infinitely worse, Mandarin is a tonal language. In effect, the same pinyin word has four totally different meanings depending on the intonation indicated.

Chinese is spoken by more than 20 percent of the people in the world. But while studying it at Beijing Language and Culture University, I often wondered how Chinese children ever learn to speak. Generally, I felt like a child, or at least deeply humbled. But on those rare occasions when I could read a sign or tell a cashier I didn't have any small change I felt like Alexander the Great at the gates of Persepolis.

Needless to say, you can't learn Chinese in a few months, but spending a semester in BLCU's short-term, accelerated program struck me as a good way to get to know Beijing, which had proved elusive on an earlier visit chiefly because I couldn't communicate.

135

BLCU specializes in teaching Chinese to overseas students. But there were many other schools in Beijing to consider, because the demand for Chinese language training is growing exponentially. The Chinese Ministry of Education estimates that 40 million people around the world study the language every year. Moreover, China's popularity among American exchange students rose 90 percent between 2002 and 2004, and just keeps growing.

A Chinese professor at my alma mater, Mount Holyoke College, recommended BLCU, a state-approved institution founded in 1962 in the leafy university district on the northwest side of Beijing. It was a perfect choice, as it turned out. Near the academic powerhouses of Peking and Tsinghua Universities, it is well-known to taxi drivers, and when I told long-time American expatriates in Beijing I was studying at BLCU, they laughed a little ruefully and said they'd started out there as well.

They were rueful, I think, because they, too, had been made to feel the fool by matriculating at the College of Intensive Chinese Training, one of several programs under the BLCU umbrella.

The school has a student body of about 15,000, a third from the PRC studying to become teachers or preparing for careers that require a foreign language. Like American college students, Chinese undergraduates at BLCU play sports, party, and call home to ask their parents for cash.

The rest of the students come from more than 120 countries around the world and generally pay their own way. They have to hit the books hard just to keep up in accelerated Chinese class, where new words, concepts, and characters are introduced relentlessly and the pedagogical approach is known as "stuffing the duck." Unprepared for the rigors, I arrived thinking I'd sit through class every weekday morning from eight to noon and spend the rest of the time tooling around Beijing.

I could have easily found an apartment off campus, but that required a residence permit from the local police. So I got a single in a dorm, figuring that living like an undergraduate would be the worst indignity I'd have to endure. I had it all backwards.

The campus, which occupies most of a city block close to the heart of Haidian around Wudaokou metro station, is an oriental ivory tower, surrounded by walls with gates locked at midnight (though pub crawlers are admitted after hours with a little pleading). It was the dreary end of a Beijing winter when I got there, so all I noticed at first was that BLCU has everything a student could need: ATMs, a library, bookstore, post office, conference center, market, hair salon, copy shop, and gymnasium with an Olympic-sized pool.

Besides the cafeteria, which serves hot Chinese meals on penitentiary-style aluminum trays for about 25 cents an entrée, there are several small restaurants specializing in foreign cuisine (though my taste buds told me that everything came from the same kitchen). I favored the LaVita Café, where I studied in the morning and went through several coffee fidelity cards. But the Muslim restaurant near the basketball courts was by far the most popular, chiefly for its delicious flatbread cooked on a round ceramic oven by a big, vicious-looking baker wielding a long wooden paddle.

Scattered around campus are 17 dorms, a few of them new high-rises, but most two-story, gray, brick buildings, vintage 1980 or so, inevitably fronted by a parking lot full of dilapidated bicycles. My dorm was number 13, near the west gate, with a front desk manned 24/7 by staff members who knew, but mostly refused to speak, English. My room, which cost about $400 a month, was on the second floor and far more comfortable than I expected.

It had walls bearing Scotch tape marks from semesters gone by, a mini-refrigerator, Internet hook-up, a hard single bed, a card-operated telephone, and a television. The TV got only state-sponsored CCTV news in English and a Korean station that aired nightly reruns of *CSI: Miami* with Korean subtitles. The private bath had an unenclosed shower dispensing water hot enough to make instant noodles.

About once a week, a washer in the faucet handle broke so I couldn't stop hot water from gushing out of the shower. By the time the plumber came, the whole room was a steam-filled sauna. And though the heating system was powerful, it was centrally operated. When I started to sweat, I asked a floor attendant how to turn it off. She rolled her eyes and, with the disdain of an upperclassman, said, "Open a window."

Most foreign students furnished their dorm rooms from the campus Friendly Store, stocking everything from bean paste to blow dryers, cheap because they were manufactured in India, a clerk told me. But wanting to make my dorm room a place I could come home to, I took a cab to the IKEA on the Fourth Ring Road, which is just like IKEAs everywhere, and visited the Panjiayuan antiques and flea market on the southeast side of town one Sunday morning. I could never have carried everything I wanted to buy there, but came away with some treasures: a bubble-shaded ceramic lamp in the shape of a Ming dynasty courtesan, a hand-painted scroll of Chinese men and caged birds, and a kitschy mantel clock, faced with a cheerful picture of Chairman Mao.

The semester began with a placement test, given in a Spartan classroom to about a dozen primarily English-speaking students. We were in the minority; young Korean-speakers predominated by a wide margin and the rest were grouped together according to their mother tongues. Instruction at BLCU starts, perforce, in the students' first languages, progressing after about a month to an all-Chinese learning environment.

I sharpened my pencils and prepared for the worst. But first, the teacher asked those of us who had never studied Chinese to raise our hands and said, "You know nothing. You can go."

So I joined the most ignorant class in BLCU's accelerated Chinese program and my status never changed. A month into the semester, I did so poorly on a practice test that it dawned on me I needed to study at least four hours a day to enjoy and benefit from class. I did all the exercises in my textbooks and made flash cards with Chinese characters on one side and pinyin on the other. The only thing I didn't do to get ahead was to hook up with a language partner, though native English speakers like me were in such hot demand that Chinese students occasionally tailed me across campus working up the courage to suggest we team up for English-Mandarin conversation exchange.

Soon I was doing better, and my classmates noticed.

They were a wonderfully mixed and motley crew from all the corners of the world where people are realizing that their futures may be inevitably tied to China.

I spoke French with Joelle, a tall young woman born in the Republic of Congo and educated in Poland. Roger, from Brazil, planned to study with a Chinese martial arts master. Michael was an E. M. Forster-esque Englishman, between jobs in Asia. Tatyana came from Vladivostok and spoke only Russian, so she used a dictionary to translate the teacher's English into her own language. Mohammed, from Egypt, had to contradict people who assumed he had a harem, and we all thought that Shinji, a Korean with a sociology degree from the University of Chicago and a build like Superman, worked for the CIA.

There were only two other students from the United States, one a Chinese-American girl who wasn't sure whether she wanted to be a writer or a dentist, the other a 30-something New Yorker whose excellence at Chinese quickly made him the class favorite. When our teacher struggled to explain the nuances of Mandarin in English, Jacob stepped in to assist her.

We were given three textbooks, published at BLCU, on Chinese grammar, listening, and speaking. Three teachers— *laoshi* in Mandarin—rotated with them. In China, the teaching profession is highly revered. I revered my instructors anyway, especially Wu *laoshi*, a thin, bespectacled woman in her 30s with an unfulfilled yen to see the world.

On a bench near my dorm, she prepped me for my role as *laoshi* in a skit my class reluctantly performed at the spring talent show. We commiserated about some of my fellow students' perpetual tardiness and obvious failure to prepare.

I told Wu *laoshi* not to worry, *bie zhaoji,* in Chinese. Our class was full of oddballs. She didn't know that word, but when I explained I got a good laugh out of her.

BLCU cleared out during Golden Week, the big spring holiday in the PRC. I went to Tibet, but got back in time to prepare for midterms. We were graded on a 100-point scale, with no curve, and I came very close to flunking.

Never mind. Winter yielded to spring, with translucent

skies and lilacs by the post office.

Who knew that Chinese lilacs smell as sweet as those in America?

Who could have predicted I'd wake up every morning on my hard single bed savoring the sound of Chinese basketballs thumping on the nearby court and the rubber-soled beat of the apparently prepubescent security force running past my window?

Who knew how much I'd cherish the time I spent at BLCU, even if all the Chinese I remember now is *bie zhaoji*?

THE INELUCTABLE ALLURE OF LOST PLACES

You expect places to stay put. Once they're on maps, they should remain there. But cartographers know hundreds of places that don't exist anymore, from the tiny Krakatoan islets of Indonesia, all but wiped out in a volcanic eruption in 1883, to the vast USSR, which made anachronisms of atlases when it disbanded several decades ago.

As Allen Carroll, chief cartographer for the National Geographic Society in Washington, D.C., once told me, "The world is very dynamic."

I would like to visit Prussia, for example, which has a long history but no longer exists on modern maps. Similarly, I want to see the majestic spires of Glen Canyon on the Colorado River in Utah, which were obliterated after the construction of Glen Canyon Dam; Tibet before the Chinese takeover; and scads of places in Eastern Europe I've read about but can't find on maps: Pomerania, Volhynia, Bukovina, Courland, Bessarabia, all of which sound to my ear like the homelands of nutty dukes and counts in Marx Brothers movies. The more gone Bessarabia is, the more I want to see it. That's the romance of places off the map.

To console myself and better understand why places aren't as permanent as I think they ought to be, I turned to geographers, who cite a variety of reasons why towns, countries, regions, and geographical features disappear from maps, even though they may remain in history books and memory.

Natural disasters such as earthquakes, floods, and volcanic eruptions have swept away such places as the Krakatoan islands and half of Santorini, now a crescent in the Aegean Sea edging the caldera of the volcano that formed the Greek island. Add to that the rising oceans that have engulfed coastal hamlets in southeastern England. When the tide goes in or out, you can still hear their church bells ring. Global warming, which is raising sea levels, imperils low-lying islands and littorals from the North Atlantic to the South Pacific.

Places appear and disappear when hydroelectric facilities are built, damming rivers and creating lakes where there were once valleys. This explains in part why such projects are increasingly controversial. Some at the radical end of the spectrum would like to see Utah's Glen Canyon Dam blown up, unleashing the once wild Colorado River and draining 186-mile-long Lake Powell.

Some people rue the construction of the Three Gorges Dam in China, which generates huge amounts of electricity and controls flooding on the Yangtze River, but also displaced or destroyed countless cities, towns, and areas of natural beauty.

Author James Dickey turned the romance of lost places into high adventure with his novel *Deliverance,* turned into an unforgettable 1972 movie, filmed on the Chattooga River between Georgia and South Carolina. In it, four weekend canoeists set off to run a river just before it's dammed. "This whole valley will be under water. But right now it's wild. . . .We really ought to go," says one of the characters in the novel, underscoring the fact that wilderness and rapids are also obliterated by dams.

Through the years, cartographers have made mistakes, showing places on maps that never existed. Such is the case with Friesland, purportedly an island southwest of Iceland that persisted on charts from 1558 to the 1660s, when cartographers decided it was mythic and consigned it to the scrap box.

Above all, politics and war change maps. East Germany and South Yemen surrendered their sovereignty in 1990; Tibet became a part of China by force in 1951. Bessarabia, bounded by the Dniester and Prut Rivers in southeastern Europe, was part of the Roman Empire, Turkey, Russia, and Romania before it changed hands again after the fall of the Soviet Union. To find where it was, you have to go to Moldavia and Ukraine.

There are 196 countries in the world, according to the United Nations. But different organizations have different criteria for defining independent countries. To qualify as an independent country in the eyes of the National Geographic Society, a nation has to declare independence, control territory, demonstrate political stability, and have international recognition.

Goodbye, Bessarabia.

I know it's still there because I think, dream, and read about it. Call me romantic. I don't care. I'm even holding out hope for Shangri-La, that lost lovely valley beyond the Karakoram Mountains where, in James Hilton's 1933 novel, *Lost Horizon*, people live on and on. It isn't long life expectancy that compels me. It's the idea that, while countries and cartographers come and go, there could be amazing places in the world that aren't on maps because we don't know they're there.

❖ 22 ❖

INTO THE SNOW GLOBE

It is 260 steps from the entrance of massive St. Isaac's Cathedral in the heart of St. Petersburg to the colonnade that encircles the base of the dome. I climbed slowly and counted. It was winter, and the stone staircase was slick with ice, ending at a high, snow-coated corner of the great Russian Orthodox church.

There, horrified, I realized that to reach the colonnade, I had to cross a metal gangplank, about 40 feet long, slung over the cathedral's sloping roof from where I stood to the dome. I steeled myself and started walking. Halfway up, I felt a blast of cold wind pluck at the gangplank like *pizzicato* on a violin string. When I reached the narrow walkway behind the colonnade, I clutched the slender handrail and tried to calm myself. Finally, I looked out and claimed the prize for having come to St. Petersburg in January: a 360-degree view of the city—its bridges, parks, golden spires, and fuming smokestacks in the suburbs writing in white on a baby blue sky.

Fulfilling fantasies is a big part of why I travel, certainly what drew me to this famous Russian city, where I imagine myself riding in a sleigh along a canal. My jet black hair is pinned in a diamond tiara and my pale, flawless shoulders draped in white fur. I have waltzed with princes, eaten caviar from crystal, lived in palaces of malachite and alabaster. My name is Anna, or Lara, or Irina. Doubtless, I read too many Russian novels at too tender an age and never stopped seeing them through rose-tinted glass, because I still sometimes imagine myself in Anna

Karenina's tiara and Dr. Zhivago's sleigh. Though my passport picture shows a middle-aged woman, my dreams reflect a beautiful Russian girl in the perfect world of a snow globe.

I could cite a score of other reasons I went to St. Petersburg in January, beginning with long-needed restoration of such vaunted sights as the Alexander Column on Palace Square, commemorating the city's 300th anniversary. I could mention the winter season at the ballet and symphony, when there is almost as much to keep a dance and music lover happy as in New York, but with more manageable crowds. I could invoke the Hermitage, surely one of the greatest art museums in the world, or say I wanted to see winter freeze shut Peter the Great's "Window on the West," a shantytown on the marshy delta of the Neva River when the czar founded it in 1703, later one of the most elegant and cosmopolitan capitals in the world.

Or I could tell the truth, that I came to St. Petersburg to realize a dream that any fool could have predicted was bound to melt like a snowflake in my hand.

Boris Pasternak's *Doctor Zhivago* is set in Moscow, not St. Petersburg, as are major parts of Leo Tolstoy's *Anna Karenina*. Anton Chekhov's *The Three Sisters* yearned for Moscow, Moscow, Moscow, which replaced Peter's imperial city to the north as the Russian capital after the abdication of the last czar and the Bolshevik rise to power in 1917. Throughout the 20th century, under the Communists, St. Petersburg went into a long, slow decline. Its opulent Italian Baroque palaces moldered; the art of the czars was sold off, stashed in damp basements or moved to Moscow; money and power fled. During World War II, an estimated 1 million civilians died in the horrific 900-day German siege. As perhaps the ultimate humiliation, the city once known as the "Venice of the North" was, in quotidian fashion, renamed Leningrad.

If anything, the fall of the Soviet Union made matters worse, though in 1991, the Russian Parliament reinstated the name Peter the Great gave the city. Economic hardship brought continued deterioration and crime, including Mafia-style shootings of politicians and the robbery of a Finnish diplomat by men in police uniforms in 2001. You couldn't drink the tap water or walk along the sidewalks of the Nevsky Prospect, the city's principal street, without falling into a crack. Though St. Petersburg often appeared on travel magazine lists of places people most wanted to visit, tourism all but evaporated. Those who came were largely on shore excursions from Baltic Sea cruise ships, viewing the city from hermetically sealed tour buses.

That's how I first visited it in the late 1990s, when I found St. Petersburg depressing for its faded look, empty streets, and hucksters of Soviet-era war medals. But dreams die hard— Peter's, mine, and, it would seem, those of Russian Federation President Vladimir Putin, who was born and raised in St. Petersburg. Putin clearly has a soft spot for the tenuous, miraculous city in Russia's frozen north, earmarking $1.5 billion for refurbishments as the city's 300th anniversary approached in 2003.

Most people visit in the summer, of course, especially for the White Nights Festival from May to July, a celebration of the arts, warm weather, and sunshine at midnight. I'm glad I went in January, even though the city of 4.8 million is nearly the same latitude as Anchorage, Alaska, and winter a time of short, dull days, frigid temperatures, blizzards, and falling icicles that kill several people every year. In Russia, they call it "General Winter" for the way it stopped invasions by Napoleon and Hitler. But if you dress warmly and embrace the cold as you would a cranky old friend, you will see St. Petersburg at its best: cracks in the Neva River, like calligraphy on white paper; parks, gardens, bridges, heroic statues beautifully blanketed in snow; canals locked in ice; people emerging from office buildings in stylish full-length fur coats. (Ask St. Petersburgers about animal rights, and they roll their eyes.)

Winter—real, white Russian winter—is a singular thing, deadly and cozy at the same time, as Pasternak described it in his poem "Winter Night," which starts: "It snowed and snowed, the whole world over; snow swept the world from end to end. A candle burned on the table; a candle burned."

St. Petersburg is the candle. If cities have seasons—Paris spring, New York fall—then winter best becomes St. Petersburg.

Visiting Russia is never a lark, no matter the season. I had Exeter International, a Florida company that specializes in travel to Eastern Europe and Russia, arrange my four-day stay, with a Russian guide and a car and driver. Though I generally prefer to be left to my own devices, this seemed wise, because I was traveling alone and don't speak Russian. For once, I didn't feel guilty about choosing an expensive place to stay and a pricey itinerary; the dream I was chasing would not be found in cheap seats or budget hotels.

Constantine Lutoshkin, my young guide, met me at the airport. He opened doors for me, made dinner reservations, carried my camera at times, and was ready with dates, statistics, facts in the Hermitage Museum and the Church of the Spilled Blood. One day in the car, we passed a stand selling red caviar blinis. Idly, I said they looked good. So Constantine made sure I got to try one before I left. (They were delicious. Salty, piping hot, perhaps the world's best street food.)

But as accommodating as Constantine was, I never really got to know him. There were off-moments when he revealed that he was about to get married, preferred Dostoevski to Tolstoy, and kept a pet snake. When I introduced political topics, such as the war in Iraq, he was unwilling to say anything that might offend. Only when I mentioned that I admired Mikhail Gorbachev, the Soviet leader who introduced *glasnost* and *perestroika* just before the collapse of the former Soviet Union, did Constantine's feelings seem to surge. Westerners like Gorbachev, he said; Russians love Putin.

We spent our first day together driving from site to site, beginning, as is appropriate, with the St. Peter and Paul Fortress on the north bank of the Neva, where Peter the Great's city took shape, first in rough wood, then in stone designed in large part by Italian architect Domenico Trezzini. Within the fortress walls are museums, a prison, military parade grounds, and a richly gilded cathedral where the floor is lined with the tombs of Romanovs, the family that ruled Russia from 1613 to 1917. Most poignant to a romantic—especially one who has read Robert K. Massie's *Nicholas and Alexandra*—were those of the last czar and czarina, imprisoned and executed in 1918 by the Bolsheviks near the Ural Mountains city of Yekaterinburg. Their remains were moved to the cathedral almost a century later in a gesture that seems to bespeak the way Russians have begun to cautiously re-embrace their imperial past.

On the riverbank, just east of the fortress, we stopped briefly at Peter the Great's simple log cabin, where the czar lived while workers wrested St. Petersburg out of the Neva swamp. It's hard to imagine, but at the beginning, the city was as mean and muddy as a Western mining camp, peopled by serfs, prisoners of war, and members of Peter's court who were forced, under protest, to move there from Moscow. In 1715, a woman was devoured by wolves in the vicinity of the Menshikov Palace on nearby Vasilevsky Island. There were no bridges over the Neva, which suited Peter, a maritime enthusiast who required St. Petersburgers to cross the many-channeled river exclusively by sailboat; only when several people died doing so did he rescind the order.

Peter, one of history's most fabled rulers, is hard to fathom, even if you spend your days touring the city he created out of nothing and reading Massie's biography of him at night, as I did. Though his education was spotty, the czar was a man of countless enthusiasms, including science, engineering, and war. As a princeling in Moscow, he played soldier with Russian troops and live ammunition, and later toured Western Europe incognito, captivated more by Dutch shipyards than by the court of the French king. Throughout his life, he routinely drank himself into stupors and was subject to embarrassing seizures, which only the Lithuanian peasant girl who became his second wife, Catherine I, seemed able to quell.

Ultimately, Peter's city grew up on the south bank of the Neva, around a shipyard now occupied by the magnificent Admiralty building. Its yellow neoclassical facade, stretching 1,335 feet along the river, bordered by parks and topped by a 218-foot gold spire, dominates the city center. Nearby are all of St. Petersburg's grandest architectural ensembles and main tourist attractions (with such notable exceptions as Peterhof and Tsarskoe Selo, imperial palaces in the suburbs).

But my time was limited, and winter weather discouraged

wandering. So—with and without my guide—I concentrated on the walkable Admiralty, where streets that recall the film version of *Dr. Zhivago* are lined by facades painted in pastels to break up winter's white monotony. There the arts, culture, society, and wealth of the czars came to full flower at the turn of 20th century.

Most likely, the black-haired woman in my Russian fantasy was coming home from a ball at the Winter Palace. Just east of the Admiralty, the palace is the historic heart of the Hermitage Museum, commissioned in the mid-18th century by Empress Elizabeth, Peter the Great's giddy daughter. The designer was Italian architect Bartolomeo Rastrelli, who, together with other artists and architects imported from Italy by the czars, put his mark all over the city. What stories those lettuce-green walls could tell of lavish balls, assignations, plots, murder, revolution. Russian director Alexander Sokurov tried to tell it all in *Russian Ark*, a movie released in 2002 that looks back at the age of the czars with more than a little nostalgia. It was filmed in one continuous take inside the Hermitage, with 850 actors and costumes galore. In the last, memorable, scene, a throng of party-goers—men in 18th-century military uniforms with epaulets and sabers, women in ball gowns, jewels, fur, and feathers—crowd down the gorgeous Jordan Staircase.

On my second day in St. Petersburg, Constantine and I entered the Hermitage near the Jordan Staircase. All white stone, red carpet, gold gilding, and Baroque sculpture, this once was an ambassadors' route, then became the path the czar took for a religious ceremony commemorating Christ's baptism in the river Jordan, for which it earned a new moniker. I spent five hours in the museum, blissfully uncrowded in winter, but it seemed no more than a minute in relation to how much there was to see. Besides historic rooms such as the 19th-century Field Marshals Hall and St. George Throne Room with its Carrara marble, the Hermitage has 3 million artworks, 5 percent of which are on display. Constantine made sure I hit the highlights: Leonardo da Vinci's tender *Benois Madonna* and Michelangelo's *Crouching Boy*, sculpted for the Medici mausoleum in Florence; more than a dozen Rembrandts, including the heart-wrenching *Return of the Prodigal Son* from about 1670; *The Dance* and *The Red Room*, by Henri Matisse; and, to me, most astonishing of all, a collection of paintings confiscated from Germany at the end of World War II, then stored away in the Soviet era, all but forgotten: one unfamiliar masterpiece after another by such early modern painters as Renoir, Van Gogh, Cezanne, and Gauguin.

In each room we passed through, there were guards, all older women in heavy sweaters and sensible shoes, thoroughly unapproachable. One sat in a rickety chair, staring out a massive dirty window overlooking Palace Square, a picture that impressed me as deeply as the Rembrandts and Van Goghs. Outside, it was snowing again, and the city seemed unreal. Only when Constantine showed me the portico of the 19th-century New Hermitage building, with a roof supported by 10 giant Atlantes, did my head start to clear. St. Petersburgers rub the feet of these giant male statues for good luck, even when their cold gray-granite toes are crusted with ice.

On our third day together, Constantine and I visited the Yusopov Palace, with a columned portico overlooking the Moika River and a diamond of a private theater; Smolny Convent, another Baroque architectural confection by Rastrelli, where the generals and administrators who helped save St. Petersburg during the German siege had their headquarters; the Russian Revival Church of the Spilled Blood, marking the place where Alexander II, who emancipated the serfs, was assassinated in 1881; and the Russian Museum on Arts Square, with its touching statue of Alexander Pushkin, Russia's Shakespeare, who died in 1837, dueling with his beautiful, vapid wife's would-be lover.

I spent one day without Constantine, picking my way along Nevsky Prospect during a flash thaw that turned St. Petersburg's busy main artery into a river of slush. As the damp seeped into my boots and socks, I shopped in Gostiny Dvor, the city's still-bustling 18th-century bazaar; had Russian champagne and smoked salmon on toast points at the Grand Hotel Europe; toured the Theater Museum near the Alexandrinsky Theater, where Chekhov's *The Seagull* premiered; and saw everything else my eyes could take in, from the colonnade of the Kazan Cathedral, recalling the one by Bernini outside St. Peter's in Rome, to the sad, shabby, touristy Literary Cafe, where Pushkin had his last demitasse.

It's taxing work seeing St. Petersburg in the winter. At the end of each day, I retired to the gracious art nouveau Hotel Astoria, on St. Isaac's Square. Sometimes I had tea in the lobby, served in exquisite blue and gold cups from the Lomonosov porcelain factory, chief china makers to the czars, or a Russian Standard vodka, the best the country has to offer, according to the Astoria bartender. Then I retreated to my chamber, which felt more like an apartment than a hotel room, decorated in a tasteful, restrained way, with a window that perfectly framed St. Isaac's Cathedral. There I rested and prepared for dinner and a concert or the theater.

Glorious, never-to-be-forgotten St. Petersburg nights ensued, the first spent at the Great Hall of the Philharmonia on Arts Square. The building, where nobles once gathered to listen to the czar, is noted for its acoustics. It played an important role during the German siege of St. Petersburg (then Leningrad), when vodka distilleries went into the business of manufacturing Molotov cocktails, circus animals were butchered for meat, and the Bronze Horseman statue of Peter the Great on Decembrists' Square was covered in sandbags to protect it from military attack. At the Philharmonia in August 1942, the starving city's spirits were raised by the debut performance of Dmitri Shostakovich's Seventh Symphony, also known as the Leningrad Symphony.

The concert hall's red velvet chairs were stained, and the coat-check lines were long. The audience had dressed for the occasion, and I had a seat close enough to the stage that I could see the first violinist's black patent leather shoes. I drank Russian champagne in the lobby at intermission. And then, of course, there was the all-Tchaikovsky program, climaxing in the Russian composer's soulful *Violin Concerto in D Major, Opus 35*. The soloist, Ukrainian-born Graf Murzha, played his violin as if quarreling with a lover.

To my mind, though, the central ingredient of a perfect

winter night in St. Petersburg is attending the ballet at the 19th-century Maryinsky Theater (known as the Kirov during the Soviet era). I caught a cab there from the Hotel Astoria and paused as I took my orchestra seat to see the czar's box behind me. Then the curtain opened and revealed a scene out of French classical landscapes by Lorrain and Poussin that I had seen in the Hermitage. The ballet was *Giselle*, with a score by Adolphe Adam and classic choreography by Marius Petipa, the ballet master of the Maryinsky from 1862 to 1903 who helped establish the company's lasting reputation for precision and elegance. Svetlana Zakharova danced the role of Giselle with awesome technical proficiency and feeling; Farukh Ruzimatov was her dramatic Count Albert. There were bouquets and countless curtain calls at the end, then the dancers were called back for 15 more minutes of adulation.

When I emerged from the theater, it was snowing, delicate flakes that seemed like a stage effect. From there, it was a five-minute walk to the Noble Nest, a restaurant in the teahouse of the Yusopov Palace with white Empire-style plasterwork, portraits of the Russian nobility, and glittering chandeliers. The staff wore uniforms like those of the dashing gentlemen in *Russian Ark*. I ordered a *kir royale*, du Barry cream soup, and Dover sole in a sauce of Pernod and trout caviar, accompanied by a split of extraordinary French Chablis, Grand Crus Les Clos, 1993. A string quartet played on the balcony. I ate slowly, savoring every delicious bite, trying to draw out the evening as long as I could.

Now, if I close my eyes, I can imagine myself there again, climbing into the taxi that returned me to my hotel, hearing the music of *Giselle* in my head, glowing with warmth and wine, feeling the feathery kiss of snow on my face. This was real, I tell myself. For one white winter night in St. Petersburg, I very nearly was the girl in the snow globe.

❖ 23 ❖

ON THE PLATEAU

My brother loves deserts, slot canyons, mesas, buttes, and treacherous dirt roads. At home in his study, he pores over US Geological Survey maps and dog ears pages in hiking books like Harvey Butchart's *Grand Canyon Treks*. Dry treatises on the archaeology and geology of the Southwest rivet him. Once, while bushwhacking through a canyon in the Santa Monica Mountains, he stopped short, fixed his gaze on a rock, and said "Ah, Conejo volcanics."

Sometimes he pulls his camping gear out on the patio: camp stove, check; sleeping bag, check; headlamp, compass, TP, check, check, check. He keeps our grandfather's rusty World War I saber under the seat of his old, white Toyota Forerunner and has a special way of setting up a tent you'd better get right if you want to go with him.

And I do, because he always takes me someplace remarkable. The year I turned 40, we did Fish and Owl Canyons in southeastern Utah, with John serving me purified water from puddles on the trail. I made him turn back on the precarious dirt road to the Maze in Utah's Canyonlands National Park, hiked with him down the Haleakala volcano on Maui, and got stuck in the Forerunner near Picacho del Diablo in Baja California.

So when he said he wanted to spend a few nights on the Powell Plateau near the North Rim of the Grand Canyon, I got a backcountry permit from the national park. Thinking we'd

155

deserve a reward after the two-night camping trip, I tried to book a cabin at the lodge, which was about to close for the season. When I found out it was full, I called every day for a week and finally got a cancellation.

I'd never been to the North Rim or heard of the Powell Plateau, but if John wanted to go there, that was all I needed to know.

Eons before my brother and I were born, seismic activity along the West Kaibab Fault in what is now northern Arizona chopped a chunk of God's country about half the size of Manhattan off the North Rim of the Grand Canyon.

You have to stand way back in your imagination to picture it, as did the 19th-century geologist Clarence Dutton when he described the region as a Grand Staircase, mounting to the tableland of central Utah on the gigantic risers of the Chocolate, Vermillion, White, Grey, and Pink Cliffs. It's a colored sand painting of a landscape as fine as any in the Southwest.

After the Powell Plateau cracked off the first step, it came to rest between the rims of the Grand Canyon on the north side of the Colorado River, which makes a big loop around it, 8,000 feet below. The top is flat, and its flanks are steeply terraced, falling away from points along the edge that overlook a canyon land unknown to most tourists.

That's partly because the Powell Plateau is reached by driving rough roads and hiking from the North Rim, visited by just a tenth of the people who see the Grand Canyon from the south. Then, too, while the warmer, dryer, less remote South Rim stays open all year, the North Rim closes when snow blocks the road around the beginning of November and re-opens in May.

But a few tough canyoneers have circled the planteau's terraces and found plentiful evidence that the mysterious Anasazi people once dwelled there. Theodore Roosevelt, cowboy fiction writer Zane Grey, and Uncle Jimmy Owens, the old canyon codger immortalized in the 1953 children's classic *Brighty of the Grand Canyon*, hunted cougars on the plateau. Colorado River explorer John Wesley Powell took the artist Thomas Moran there to paint the view from Dutton Point, a Grand Canyon advertisement.

Around 1900, William Wallace Bass, an easterner who went to the arid Southwest for his health and upon first seeing the Grand Canyon said, "It nearly scared me to death," put his money on attracting tourists to the region around Powell Plateau. He built a camp across from it on the South Rim; cobbled together old Indian and prospector paths that became the first cross-canyon route passable by horses, now the national park's tough North and South Bass Trails; put a ferry boat in the river to take visitors across the Colorado to another camp underneath the Powell Plateau, shaded by fruit trees. He knew in his gut that this was the heart of the canyon. But in 1901, the railroad reached the head of Bright Angel Trail, 30 miles east, putting Bass out of business.

I flew, and John drove the Forerunner, loaded with gear, from L.A. to Las Vegas, a good staging point for trips into the canyon lands of Utah and Arizona. He's logged 245,000 chassis-battering miles on that vehicle, and I don't trust it. So I arranged to rent an SUV at the airport, where John met me.

When the lady at the check-in counter said we could upgrade to a Hummer for $10 a day more, John's ears got as big as a mule deer's. Driving a Hummer on an abominable dirt road is the stuff of his fantasies and the price was unbeatable.

So it was that we began our Powell Plateau adventure like a pair of rap stars, cruising down the Vegas Strip in an H3.

Early the next morning, we were on our way to St. George, Utah, where we'd turn east toward the North Rim, with the Vermillion Cliffs at one shoulder and the Arizona Strip at the other. But I got a speeding ticket on Interstate 15 in the gorge of the Virgin River. The cars ahead of me were going faster, so I'm sure I was pulled over because of the flashy Hummer.

After that I took it slow, even though John kept telling me to hurry up or we'd never make it to the plateau by dark. The rest of the time he toyed with the H3's accessories—heated seats, satellite radio, a GPS unit that didn't recognize the town of Jacob Lake, Ariz., where North Rim visitors turn south to the park.

We stopped at the Kaibab National Forest ranger station in Fredonia, Arizona, where I got imprecise directions to the

Powell Plateau trailhead, reached from a turnoff on Arizona State Highway 67 about 20 miles short of the North Rim lodge. From there, we had to find our way over a network of unpaved forest roads that lead west to a series of secluded Grand Canyon overlooks on the ragged south edge of the Kaibab Plateau, among them Swamp Point, where we'd park the Hummer and start hiking.

To see us together, you wouldn't necessarily know that my brother and I are actually quite fond of one another. I chatter annoyingly. He treats me like a galley slave. But on our little adventures in the great outdoors we usually rediscover that we appreciate some of the same things, including peak experiences handed out by Mother Nature.

She was generous that October afternoon. The aspens on the road to the North Rim had turned a bright, blazing canary yellow. Suddenly, we realized why the lodge was full. Fall comes to the North Rim in a geologic nanosecond, quickly whipped away by high winds and early snowfall. But if you're lucky enough to be there at exactly the right moment, as we were, you will see an autumn display that blows the red maples of New England out of the water.

Along the way, John and I also saw evidence of man's efforts to control the fires that regularly gut big tracts of Ponderosa pine on the Kaibab Plateau. Blazes used to be suppressed in the park and adjacent national forest. But about 20 years ago, there was a dawning realization that fire is a natural part of the ecosystem, clearing out highly flammable undergrowth and thinning the trees, leaving only the hardiest Ponderosas to grow into goliaths. Conflagrations that threaten developed areas and irreplaceable sites are still vigorously battled, but others are allowed to burn, while carefully monitored. On occasion, prescribed fires are set to keep the forest healthy.

The trouble is, you can't predict fire. Some North Rim road shoulders were seared on June 25, 2006, when sudden high winds stoked a closely watched, lightning-ignited fire out of control, setting the crown of the forest alight, closing the lodge, and consuming 40,000 acres of Kaibab Ponderosas in a single night. After a fire like that, a new crop of brush and trees claim squatters' rights in the cleared spaces, including beautiful intruders like the aspen.

At first, we overshot the Swamp Ridge Road turnoff, ending up at Fire Point, where we met a couple in a camper with two chocolate Labs who said it had rained the day before. That was important information. The Powell Plateau is a lightning trap. Backpackers die in Grand Canyon electrical storms, and there's no expert agreement about how to take cover from them.

Back on the right track, we saw pond-size puddles in the road. But the sun was out and the H3 plowed right through them, though we had to stop when we saw a bison slurping from a pothole, part of a herd imported to Arizona around 1900 and cross-bred with cattle that had escaped onto the Kaibab, degrading trails and water sources. Some years ago the national park tried unsuccessfully to eradicate them, so travelers on Kaibab Forest roads sometimes still have bison encounters.

Swamp Point turned out to be an exposed, 7,565 foot shelf of Kaibab limestone that would make a good place to shoot a Jeep commercial. It looks over White Creek and North Bass Trail on their way to the basement of the Grand Canyon. I couldn't see the Colorado River from there, but John pointed to a saddle of land below the point, where there was an old national park cabin, and the landmass on the far side. "That's the Powell Plateau," he said.

By then it was already five o'clock. But we figured we could make it 800 feet down to the Muav Saddle, cross the canyon, and then climb another 900 feet on a clearly visible trail that switchbacks over the terraced northeast flank of the plateau: about two and a half miles, all told. We did it in a little over an hour, pitched our tents in the twilight and had freeze-dried chili mac for dinner. We'd been hiking in shirtsleeves, but John said I'd better bundle up for the night. It was going to get cold. It could even snow.

At 7:30, I went to bed in three pairs of Long Johns, a hooded sweatshirt, jacket, gloves, socks, and my sleeping bag. Even so, I felt like I was sleeping on ice.

No matter how well prepared you are, you take a calculated risk when going into the wilderness. John is an experienced backpacker with a high risk threshold. Mine is so low that a falling pine cone can make me panic. Plus, I'd been reading *Deep Survival*, by Laurence Gonzales, which uses neuroscience and true stories of disasters to explain who dies in the wilderness and why.

But the next morning, I felt safe and cozy on the plateau. The birds were singing and the sun was rising in a cloudless sky. Once we packed up, John and I followed the teasing Dutton Point trail through golden meadows where daisies lingered. Unmaintained and only occasionally blazed, it often lost us by petering out. After thrashing around a bit, we'd find it again.

But maybe we were too busy looking at the bizarrely shaped, blackened husks of Ponderosas—ghost trees, my brother called them—selected for death by lightning. Most North Rim fires are started by lightning, and the plateau's remoteness has made it a testing ground for the let-burn strategy of forest management. As a result, the top is a rare example of an almost virgin Ponderosa pine forest, much thinner than you'd expect for a Western forest primeval.

Around noon, we made a new camp on the edge of the plateau, with my open-sided tent-tarp looking into the canyon, lazed around in the sunshine, and then walked a few miles to Dutton Point. When we reached the edge John went first. "Come on," he yelled back. "It's like a dance floor out here."

I crawled, hardly daring to look up. But when I did I forgot I was on an 7,500 foot rock ledge. The view was magnificent, at least 180 degrees of prime Grand Canyon panorama wrapped around the southeast corner of the Powell Plateau, with the Colorado River far below, pushing west to Lake Mead after its long meander through the big ditch. We could see everything: the South Rim, clearly lower than the North; 6,242-foot Masonic Temple with its razorback ridge leading to Fan Island butte; King Arthur Castle and Galahad Point; even white water in what we deduced to be the Colorado River's Serpentine Rapids.

Only when the shadows lengthened did we leave the ledge. Back at camp we ate dinner and went to bed, mostly in silence. There wasn't much to say after a day like that.

It still amazes me to think about how fast things changed.

I started hearing the wind in the middle of the night. It sounded like a vacuum cleaner. By the time I got up, the sky was a bowl of boiling chili mac.

Without saying a word, John and I knew we had to get off the exposed plateau. He could scarcely believe how efficiently I packed up, but as Gonzales says in *Deep Survival*, fear sometimes makes people focus. I admit I was afraid, knowing that weather, not mountain lions, is the chief predator on Powell Plateau.

We left at 6:30 AM and made good time on the trail until we stopped seeing blazes. At first we followed the plateau's east rim, thinking it would inevitably lead us to the take-off point for the cross-canyon route to Swamp Point, where we had left the Hummer. But it didn't—no matter how hard we bushwhacked through scrub oak, crossed dry drainages, and looked for familiar ghost trees.

Finally, John did a hard, but very smart thing. He made us backtrack to the east rim and then walk west across the plateau, figuring we'd have to cross the trail on the way.

The sky was even uglier than before, and I was deciding that I'd lived a good life, but was ready to let go. At about that point, John said, "I just don't see how we could have missed the trail."

Then I looked down and said, "I think it's here."

After that, we got off the plateau in the knick of time. We heard the first thunder bolt climbing up from the Muav Saddle, and when we reached Swamp Point it started to pour. My clothes were sweaty-cold, so I was happy for the H3's heated seats and the way it couldn't be thwarted by deluge on Swamp Ridge Road.

At the national park checkpoint on Arizona State Highway 67, the attendant gave us a big smile when we said we'd come from Powell Plateau. Then the front desk clerk at the lodge put us in a cabin with a propane fireplace overlooking the canyon. While waiting for it to be cleaned, we ate lunch in the dining room, feeling way more righteous than the elder hostelers who'd taken up most of the rooms.

But I loved the way they slept in their name-tagged jogging suits on the south porch of the lodge and attended ranger talks on Grand Canyon geology. John and I ate well, napped hard, and cheated at National Park Monopoly while we were there. Meanwhile, the lodge tucked up for winter in 70-mile-an-hour winds.

A good trip usually has its panic and bliss. You go for the one and learn from the other. You get back in touch with matters elemental and remember who in the wide world you can count on.

Powell Plateau was one for the scrapbook. But there will be others. John isn't going to run out of places to see in the Southwest anytime soon and I'll go with him as long as I can lift a backpack.

❖ 24 ❖

PROUST AND TRADER JOE'S

For those of us who love to travel, it is a very sad thing when the trips are over and memories fade. I take plenty of pictures when I'm traveling; they remind me of where I've been and what I've seen. But they don't always bring back the experience of being in a place, and they are a nuisance to keep organized. Then, too, I'm haunted because they don't capture small, mundane, easy-to-forget things, such as brief encounters or the smell of tropical rain.

Happily, many memories can be reclaimed by doing something everyone does about once a week: grocery shopping. That's what I was up to one Saturday morning, though never in a million years would I have expected to be transported to an inn outside Oxford, England, in the breakfast food aisle at Trader Joe's. But there on the shelf I found the key to a travel memory in a box of Weetabix, a low-sodium, high-fiber English cereal made (according to a notice on the box) "By Appointment to Her Majesty The Queen." I cared about none of that the first time I saw Weetabix in England, because I was on my honeymoon.

My husband and I had slept in, and I now clearly remember how the mistress of the B & B rapped imperiously on the door to our room—decorated in a ghastly shade of pink, with mawkish fake flowers, ruffles, and bows—to tell us that we'd miss the morning meal altogether if we didn't get up. With all the genteel airs of a character in the BBC comedy *Fawlty Towers*, she served us Weetabix in fine china bowls as if it were tea at the Savoy. The cereal got soggy as we sat, looking at guidebooks and giggling behind her back.

In itself, the memory means nothing. But I am happy to have it, if for no other reason than that it proves that what is lost can, quite unexpectedly, be found. "The past is hidden somewhere . . . beyond the reach of intellect, in some material object. And it depends on chance whether or not we come upon this object before we ourselves must die"—or so said Marcel Proust in a famous passage from *Swann's Way*, when the narrator of the novel remembers something from the distant past by taking a bite of a tea-soaked Madeleine.

More and more, it seems to me that food is the material object that unlocks travel memories best. For instance, I was in heaven when I recently found *pastis*—the licorice-flavored liqueur I'd made a habit of drinking one summer in southern France—on the menu at a restaurant in the Napa Valley. My mother couldn't scoop a spoon into a ripe papaya without smelling orchids and remembering her first trip to Hawaii as a young woman. And at one Thanksgiving dinner, my sister, a Japan scholar, commenced the festivities with cocktails and *sembei* rice crackers packaged so beautifully that they could be pearls, reminding us all of the summer we had visited her while she was studying in Tokyo.

For me, this is reason enough to roam the aisles at Trader Joe's (never mind the bargains), where the in-store circular is known as *Trader Joe's Fearless Flyer* and there are cartons and jars imported from all over the world: McCann's Irish Oatmeal, made at a factory outside Dublin founded more than a century ago; pure maple syrup from French Canada; Zenith brand stuffed fig leaves (with a label in Greek); and an intriguing boxed mix for Dassant's Italian Orange Dessert Cake (add a few ingredients, stir and you're in Palermo or Capri).

Most of the products bear the company's label no matter where they're from, because Trader Joe's often contracts directly with producers to distribute olive oils, frozen fish, nuts, and the like. Their buyers are dispatched all over the globe to find affordable foods and beverages—one looking for snacks in

Japan, another searching for fresh produce in Chile, smelling cheese in Ireland, or tasting shrimp in Vietnam. Friendships develop between buyers and the producers they visit overseas. Annette Davidson, who keeps the cereals in stock, thinks that part of what keeps people coming back to Trader Joe's is that they find foods there—like Weetabix and McCann's oatmeal—that make them think of places they've visited.

Recently, I found a jar of cornichons—which, minced in tuna salad, evoke France—and some morello cherry jam made in Israel.

For me, a little of that on an English muffin is just like one of Proust's Madeleines—taking me back to childhood summers when my family vacationed on the shores of Lake Michigan near Grand Traverse Bay. On the way there, we stopped at orchards and filled the floor of our red Chevy station wagon with cartons of fresh cherries. My mother made cherry pie, and my brother drank cherry juice. One day I almost drowned in a swimming pool, and, on the beach, my father found a handful of rare Petoskey rocks. How could I ever have forgotten all that, and why didn't I figure out sooner that I only needed to reach for a jam jar to get it back?

❖ 25 ❖

SLIPPIN' DOWN TO THE SEASIDE

The bicycle has always struck me as the perfect way to travel—cheaper than driving, faster than walking, and easier to manage than a horse. I don't own a bike and am hardly fit for the Tour de France. Still, that hasn't stopped me from dreaming about a cycling trip.

But the logistics always seemed daunting: deciding where to go; renting a bike; plotting a safe, scenic route; and figuring out how in the world to carry the gear. Occasionally, I'd send for brochures describing package cycling tours—through Tuscany or the Loire Valley, with bikes and equipment, the services of a guide, accommodations, and daily luggage transfers included. But the prices left me winded.

Then I happened upon a booklet published by the Irish Tourist Board called *Walking and Cycling Ireland* while planning a trip to Ireland. It listed a number of cycle-tour companies that offer just the sort of trip I had in mind, at reasonable prices, with bikes, helmets, panniers, breakdown equipment, vouchers for booked overnight stays in B & B's and luggage transfers, all costing about $400 a person for seven days. Some were scheduled group tours, but the ones I was most interested in sent cyclists into the Irish countryside on their own, guided by route descriptions and maps. In summer, destinations include the Ring of Kerry, the Dingle Peninsula, and Connemara. I chose a tour of County Clare, in the west, offered by Irish Cycle Hire because Clare is close to Shannon Airport, not too hilly, and scenically blessed—with shimmering strands and the dramatic Cliffs of Moher bordering it to the west; ruined castles, the Aran Islands, a wild, rock-encrusted region called the Burren at its heart; and all the cockles and mussels of Galway Bay to the north.

The tour started and ended in the market town of Ennis on the River Fergus. In all, the route covered about 100 miles, mostly along two-lane country roads, with stays at four B & Bs, each about 25 miles from the other, including a farm near the spa town of Lisdoonvarna, where you get to settle in for two nights. Nothing too taxing—which was one of the inducements I used on my sister Martha to get her to come along. In early May, she flew from Washington, D.C., to Shannon, where she was met by a driver who took her straight to our first night's B & B, about a mile west of Ennis. I took the train to Ennis from Dublin, where I'd spent the week obsessing about the chill, drizzly weather. I asked everyone I met when they thought fair days would come, and got my favorite answer from a man at a laundromat who said, "Ireland's a grand country. Rain is the only fault in it."

The temperature was about 45 degrees and the skies fitful when I reached Ennis on a Sunday afternoon. Next to the train station was a small shed housing the Irish Cycle Hire depot, and in the parking lot there was a woman wearing purple rain pants making crazy circles on a bike. On second look, I recognized her as someone I'd known all my life—my sister, testing out an 18-gear Shimano mountain bike. We'd requested women's models, but there were only men's on hand; and though the bikes were in reasonably good condition, and rode just fine, Martha ultimately found herself missing the Peugeot City Express parked on her porch back home. Still, the young depot manager obliged us by raising the seats, helped us strap on our panniers, and gave us a B & B voucher booklet and map. The map was so lacking in detail that I never referred to it again, and I had to call a cab to get my luggage taken to the B & B. We encountered a few more glitches during the tour. But only the finicky would dwell on them, because the minute the Sisters Spano put their tires to the road, spring came to County Clare. The sun shone, wildflowers bloomed, birds sang.

Martha took me on a warm-up ride around Ennis, for centuries a stronghold of the O'Brien family, which gave Ireland a hero: Brian Boru, who briefly united the island's squabbling Celtic clans to drive out the Vikings in 1014. I bought a fistful of maps at the tourist information center. After that, we visited the lovely ruins of Ennis Friary, built for Franciscans by Turlough O'Brien around 1300, and then moved next door to Cruise's Pub. Beside the fireplace there, Martha ordered seafood chowder, I had a smoked salmon sandwich, and we both embarked on a long voyage of discovery into the peaty, smoky realm of Irish whisky, with a shot each of Paddy's.

Gaily we pedaled by the River Fergus where swans glided, and alongside emerald greens, golfers deliberating even in the dying light. Just beyond the last hole lay our B & B, a modern suburban home called Eyredemesne. Our spacious, pink-walled room was at the back on the second floor, with two double beds, a private bath, and a television we never turned on.

Truth be told, Martha and I both regretted that all the B&Bs we booked were of somewhat charmless recent construction. But they all had positive features, chiefly their proprietresses— flinty, handsome Irishwomen who were excellent conversation-alists and breakfast chefs. Indeed, morning chats with them often resulted in late starts, and hot breakfasts were abundant enough to provide the fixings for a picnic lunch. Routinely, we made sandwiches out of leftover bacon and brown bread, supplemented by black currant juice and Cadbury hazelnut chocolate bars we bought on the way.

Routinely, too, we saw stirring sights and had serendipitous meetings with the Irish, like the aged farmer in muddy Wellies whom we met on our first day out near the top of the highest mountain in the area, Slieve Callan (1,400 feet). Noting that we were somewhat breathless from the ascent, he gestured to Clare's Atlantic coast, which rolled away to the west, dappled by patches of flowering gorse, and assured us that we'd "go slipping down to the seaside now." Just as he promised, it was an easy spin to An Gleann, our next B&B, which lay along the main road about half a mile outside the resort village of Milltown Malbay. When we arrived in the early afternoon, the mistress, who'd been sheltering cyclists for some years, showed us to our comfortable, private-bath double on the second floor (with a hot pot for making coffee and tea), and then got straight to the point. "How're your bums?" she asked.

Actually, our bums were rather sore. But that didn't stop us from riding to a beautiful beach called Spanish Point, about two miles south of Milltown Malbay, and then tucking into fresh cod and trout dinners at the Ocean View Restaurant in town. Afterward, we'd have liked to stay around to hear west country pipers and fiddlers play in Milltown Malbay's pubs, but we didn't relish riding home along narrow, shoulderless roads in the dark. Our night life was similarly curtailed throughout the trip, since all our B & Bs were some distance from the nearest towns. Though with all the fresh air and exercise I was getting, after about 10, nothing appealed to me more than the prospect of bed.

On Tuesday morning, we pedaled north along the coast. My sister set the pace to the hamlet of Lahinch on Liscannor Bay and waved to every sheep she passed. At an antiques shop there called Inne, I admired a Georgian oak chair from 1780. And across the street in the Kenny Woollen Mills outlet, I bought an Irish sweater. It was a machine-made black and white pullover in which I felt I cut a fine figure, standing 700 feet above the Atlantic Ocean on the Cliffs of Moher.

Then we did a bit more slipping down to Lisdoonvarna, set amid rolling hills on the Aille River, where we found the Spa Wells Health Center, a pleasant, old-fashioned, garden-circled spot with sulfur water from a spring called Gowlaun on tap. The center was still getting ready for the season, but a nice young man showed us the bathhouse and a rather strange set of battery-powered shock plates, for use in a sulfur bath, attached to a person's feet and back. The little charge emitted is said to be a muscle relaxant. But Martha and I relaxed instead over a couple of John Power whiskies, some seafood chowder, and a delicious plate of mackerel pâté at the cozy Roadside Tavern in town, before cycling about two miles north to my favorite B & B—a farmhouse called Slieve Elva, near a prehistoric standing stone and the medieval ruins of Kilmoon Church.

Our room at Slieve Elva wasn't substantially different from any of the others we stayed in. But I liked watching television in the parlor with the young Donnellan boys and cutting my own sod from a mountainside bog. It came out of the ground looking like chocolate.

On our rest day, Martha and I biked about five miles east to the pretty fishing village of Doolin, where we caught a ferry called the Happy Hooker to Inisheer, the closest Aran Island to the mainland, and the smallest at about six square miles. There's a lovely, white-sand beach at the harbor there, with the ruins of an eighth-century church and fourteenth-century O'Brien castle above. But it is Inisheer's dizzying maze of stone walls that strike a visitor most—with every cow the ruler of its own little rock-lined pasture.

On we rode the next day, into the Burren, where low hills with names like Cappanawalla and Poulacapple are coated with limestone and cut by furrows that nourish gem-like blue gentians in the spring. Near the bottom of Corkscrew Hill, we had morning tea with homemade scones on elegant white china at Gregans Castle Hotel, and, about a half-mile south of the village of Ballyvaughan on Galway Bay, toured a 16th-century fortified tower house called Newtown Castle. At the Monk's Pub in Ballyvaughan, we found what my sister considered the trip's most distinctive seafood chowder. And I'd have liked to steal the sheepdog who followed us all the way from there to the twelfth-century ruins of Corcomroe Abbey near Bell Harbour.

But he ran away just before we reached Clareview House, about three miles east of Kinvara—a lovely, two-story farmhouse undergoing renovation at the time of our visit. Which is why our second-floor double had nice new carpeting and pink wallpaper, but no wastebaskets, towel racks, or hot water.

After riding bikes all day, the plumbing situation came as a major blow. But the lady of the house did her best to make up for it by dropping us in town for dinner and taking us home afterward. The next morning, she gave us directions to Coole Park, about seven miles south just outside Gort, and offered to meet us there in the early afternoon, to put our bikes in the trunk of her car, and drive us back to Ennis. After some deliberation, we took her up on the idea—not because we were too tired to cycle the last 20-mile leg of the trip, but because we had been routed along the busy main highway connecting Galway and Ennis.

The plan gave us more time to tour Coole Park, the site of a great house owned by Lady Augusta Gregory around the turn of the 19th century. The house was demolished in 1941, but the exquisite grounds remain, shaded by graceful woods and bordered by a lake, where Lady Gregory's friend, William Butler Yeats, saw a flock of swans "drift on the still water, mysterious, beautiful."

Back in Ennis that night, Martha and I drifted from one pub to the next, drinking our favorite Irish whisky, Jameson 1780, and discussing the tour. We both thought that it would have made more sense to route us back to Ennis via the Burren villages of Kilfenora or Corofin, where we could have spent our next-to-last night. But, all things considered, we had a good trip—chiefly due to the brilliant weather. So we toasted that, and sisterhood, and Kirkpatrick MacMillan, the inventor of the modern bicycle.

COOKING WITH CAPERS

That's it, I thought, emptying a plastic bag of capers, the last of the little hoard I'd brought home from Lipari. I put one in my mouth and rolled it around. Its flavor was earthier and more intense than an olive, and its essence took me back to the island flung into the middle of the Tyrrhenian Sea, where the parched, volcanic soil yields little but capers and where my Italian grandfather was born.

In *The Odyssey*, Lipari was the domain of Aeolus, king of the winds. Capital of a seven-island archipelago north of Sicily called the Lipari, or Aeolian, Islands, it was the source of shiny, black obsidian for the Mediterranean basin in the neolithic age; a Greek colony; the scene of naval battles between Rome and Carthage during the Punic Wars and plunder for North African pirates; and a place of exile for opponents of Mussolini in the 1920s.

That's about the gist of what can be said of Lipari. Just 13 square miles, with a population of 13,000, it isn't Tuscany or Rome. And it isn't easy to get to. There's no airport, which means you must take a ferry or hydrofoil from Naples, Sicily, or Reggio di Calabria, at the toe of the Italian boot. My family and I left from Naples, having spent a week on the Amalfi coast, a long-needed reunion for the dispersed remnants of the little clan.

We were in VIP class on the hydrofoil, which meant we got packaged sandwiches. But the air conditioning wasn't working; passengers were allowed outside only on a tiny deck clogged with smokers; and there was just one bathroom. When we reached the Aeolians, all but comatose after five hours at sea, the hydrofoil stopped at four of the outer islands before landing at Lipari.

First, Stromboli—a perfect volcanic cone rising out of a flat, glassy sea; it occasionally erupts so violently that the entire island has to be evacuated. During filming of the 1949 movie *Stromboli*, directed by Roberto Rossellini, there was an eruption of another sort: a scandalous love affair between the Italian director and Ingrid Bergman, his then-married leading lady.

While serving in the Navy during World War II, my father passed the island, the northernmost in the Aeolian chain, during a storm at night. "I was the officer in charge of the ship," he wrote in his journal. "As much as I tried to head the vessel away, it was being driven inexorably toward the light on a small island. The next morning, I went into the chart room and realized that the light was on one of my father's islands."

My father would visit Lipari with my mother on vacation nearly 50 years later, in 1990, seeking evidence of his father, whom he'd hardly known. Giovanni Spano came to New York in the early 20th century, married my grandmother, had three children with her, and then divorced. They remarried some years later, but by then, it was the 1950s, and my father had started a family of his own in the Midwest. In that time and place, people wanted to blend in, not expose their ethnic roots. All we knew of our grandfather was where he came from and that he died in 1973.

But an imagined Lipari lived in my mind. As the boat rounded Lipari, I pointed out to my niece, the village of Quattropani on the island's port-less northwestern coast where my grandfather—her great-grandfather—was born. We made another stop on bleak, crater-pocked Vulcano, just south of Lipari, separated from the bigger island by a narrow strait.

"This is what Santorini and Rhodes must have been like 50 years ago," my brother said. Even from a distance, the Aeolians seemed to me quintessentially Italian, not Greek—a distinction similar, perhaps, to the one between capers and olives.

❖

After the long trip from Naples, nobody wanted to leave dry land anytime soon. But the day after our arrival, an excursion boat captain convinced us that the best way to see the Aeolians is from the water; like California's Channel Islands, they are not a place of gentle meetings between earth and sea. The best spots—deserted coves and pebble beaches—lie beneath massive, eroded cliffs and can't be reached by land. For this reason, sailors favor the islands, which are the setting for Michelangelo Antonioni's 1960 *L'Avventura*, a stunningly beautiful film about a young woman who goes missing on a yachting holiday.

There were no such disasters with Captain Marco, who showed us grottoes, rock arches, and volcanic plugs, or towers, stranded off southwestern Lipari, then crossed the strait to Vulcano, where we anchored in a cove with yellow broom spilling down its sides. We swam there, blissfully, plunging from the side of the boat into clean, cool, buoyant saltwater.

The village of Gelso, on the southern side of Vulcano, had a family-style restaurant and a little harbor and pier from which we could see Sicily on the southern horizon. There, salt-scrubbed and sun-varnished, we sat down to lunch: first Vulcano cheese with hot red pepper, then heaping dishes of squid and eggplant spaghetti, followed by little goblets of sweet, sticky malmsey wine, made from sun-cured Aeolian grapes. A memorable feast, truly family style.

The next day, we toured Lipari by van with an English-speaking guide, Pasquale, a professorial-looking man whose manners were polished to a sheen. When we stopped at a viewpoint near the crater of Monte Pilato, he pointed out a rock with a glistening black streak of obsidian, which ancient humans used as a cutting implement. Farther up the eastern coast, we saw hillsides of white pumice, like ski runs, bottoming out at quarries near the shore.

On the northwestern corner of the island, we stopped at a farm stand by the highway, looking across the strait to the neighboring island of Salina, the setting for 1994's *Il Postino*. Everyone found something to buy: bottled sardines, sun-dried tomatoes, cactus jelly, homemade biscotti, obsidian jewelry, and capers, the immature buds of a bushy plant that loves niches and crags all over the Aeolians. These were different from the capers I'd purchased back at home in glass jars, preserved not in oil, but in local sea salt.

We told Pasquale that we were there because of our grandfather and that we especially wanted to see Quattropani.

"Other families have come looking for their roots," he said solemnly. "They all find something."

My grandfather's town was just down the road, with houses pinioned to the hills and views so beautiful it was hard to imagine how anyone could leave. Quattropani has just one grocery store and restaurant, one old and one new church, and a cemetery strung with lights that make it look a little like a fairground after the circus. There were pictures of deceased loved ones on crypt fronts and tombs, among them many Spanos—Giovannis, Giuseppes, Antoninos—but none we knew.

The old church nearby is the destination of an annual Liparian pilgrimage honoring Sicily's Santa Maria della Catena in early September. It's fronted by a blank piazza, with benches looking across the strait to Salina, and has green doors and a Byzantine dome. I was unnerved when I saw it, because the church and piazza reminded me of the setting for the profoundly troubling last scene in *L'Avventura*, in which a man and woman—friends of the boating-accident victim, now lovers—gaze resignedly into Mediterranean nothingness. And then we met an old woman right out of the Antonioni movie, the church custodian, sitting on a bench, with the gravitas of a Pieta and dyed, thinning hair. She said there was a Spano who ran a florist shop in Lipari town and told us stories of our Quattropani kin, including a cousin several times removed named Francesca, whose love letters from a swain in America were confiscated by her maiden aunt, scuttling their budding romance and consigning Francesca to life-long spinsterhood.

I don't know what people who go looking for their roots expect to find. We didn't get to know Grandpa Spano despite the time we spent on his island. But for me, there was the joy of being in a place that somehow felt right, with my family. We wandered the cobblestone alleys of Lipari town, decorated with drying laundry, shopped for custom-made sandals and old prints, then climbed to the Aeolian Museum atop the acropolis, a Gibraltar-like rock that has been inhabited since the fourth century BC. Its tombs and pottery testify to wave after wave of immigration from Sicily, Greece, the Italian mainland, Normandy, and Spain. From the Greek era, there is an extraordinary cache of theatrical masks and figurines, some of which have told scholars all they know about plays by Sophocles, Euripides, Aristophanes, and Menander that have been lost in text form.

On the last night of our family reunion, we went to Da Filippino, which guidebooks said was the best restaurant in town. We ordered a bottle of Sicilian Chardonnay, then looked at the catch of the day, displayed on a nearby table—sea urchin, swordfish, squid, tuna. I started with antipasto Liparota, a kind of Italian sushi wrapped in pecorino cheese, chose a dish of Hades black squid ink risotto as a main course, and then had homemade chocolate tartufo as a *dolce*. The dinner lasted forever, or until little glasses of malmsey wine came around. Everyone in my little family band was happy.

There's a postscript, though, because my brother John and I stayed on for a few days. We'd often traveled together and like the same things. So after the heat of the day had broken late one afternoon, we walked around the southern point of the island to the Geophysical Observatory, where scientists observe seismic activity in the Mediterranean. John did some amateur geology on the edge of a cliff nearby, while I sat on a rock with my eyes closed.

Another day, while wandering along Lipari's main street, Corso Vittorio Emanuele, we happened upon a florist shop and stopped in. A small, sturdy, dark-haired woman behind the counter was wrapping flowers for a customer. When she finished, I asked in broken Italian if her name was Spano. She looked blank for a moment, then said she was Francesca di Spano, with the accent on the last syllable. We told her we were Spanos, with the accent on the first syllable, from the United States. At that, she called her teenage daughter, Moira, who spoke some English, from the back of the shop. When she heard we were the grandchildren of Giovanni Spano, who left Lipari for America in 1906, she had no doubt we were related through our common great-grandfather, Antonino di Spano. I'd have been skeptical, because when my parents went to Lipari in 1990, they also met Spanos of uncertain relation, who took them around the island in an antiquated Willys jeep. Could there be, I wondered, a small cottage industry on Lipari in Spano roots tours?

But Moira drew up a family tree, and there was no mistaking the resemblance between Francesca and my father's sister. When Francesca's son, Marco, appeared, there was no mistaking his hairline. It was my dad's.

The Spanos took the Spanos to lunch at L'Orchidea, a family place in the village of Pianoconte, west of the port. The young wife of the owner, a second-generation Italian American immigrant to Lipari from Brooklyn, served as our translator, while also presenting us with plates of delicious homemade pasta and fresh fish. After lunch, we went to Francesca's house in Quattropani, surrounded by gardens and vineyards, and then back to the local cemetery to find what we'd missed on the previous visit.

Francesca stopped at the tomb of her father, Antonino Giuseppe Spano, my Grandpa Spano's nephew, and kissed his picture. Then she led us to our great-grandfather's crypt, bearing a picture of the Spano scion, who wore a waxed handlebar mustache.

What all this means to me is still hard to say, except that it's good to know who my great-grandfather was and the right way to pronounce my name; that part of me comes from an enchanted island in the Tyrrhenian Sea; and how to cook with capers.

❖ **27** ❖

ON MY OWN

At a famous dumpling restaurant in the Chinese city of Xi'an, the maître d' told me he couldn't seat me because I was alone. Feeling stubborn—not to mention hungry—I waited in the foyer for 45 minutes, watching waiters push through the kitchen door carrying oversized bottles of beer, tureens of steaming soup, and platters of dumplings so beautifully decorated that they looked like bonbons. Finally, a large round table opened up, which I insisted on taking. There I sat, sampling each delicious course as it came, surrounded by seven empty chairs.

The problem isn't just that the Chinese don't cook for one; when you travel alone, hardly anyone does. The world is a feast spread for two at the very least. Aboard cruise ships, at spas, and on package tours, the rule is almost always one room, two people. Single occupancy is allowed, but usually a supplement is charged, and although one does sometimes find hotels with lower-priced single rooms, they are usually the dreariest, smallest, worst-located accommodations in the house—in basements or overlooking air shafts. Furthermore, when you travel *à deux* you can split ancillary expenses, like car rentals— surely a convincing argument for finding a companion.

Sometimes I do, and not entirely for budgetary reasons. Some trips, like the bicycle tour of County Clare, Ireland, I took with my sister one spring, are simply more do-able with someone else along. And I'm no daredevil, so I recognize that there are things I shouldn't attempt on my own, like back-

179

packing through isolated valleys of the Anti-Atlas Mountains in Morocco. For this reason, I joined a tour group headed there without knowing a soul—least of all the roommate the English tour operator assigned me. Sharing quarters with a stranger struck me as dicey, but as luck would have it, she turned out to be a funny and considerate Scot I'm happy to count as a friend and wouldn't mind traveling with again.

After all, it is nice to have company. This fact was driven home to me in China, on an overnight train from Beijing to Xi'an. There I met a young American couple, sitting across from me. I arrived in the sleeping compartment minutes before the train pulled out, overheated from lugging my bags down the platform and discombobulated because I'd gone to the wrong station to catch the train. To get to the right one in time, I'd had to pay an outlandish sum of money to a cab driver, who gleefully ran red lights all across Beijing while I clutched the dashboard and prayed. When I told my fellow travelers about it, they said that they'd almost gone to the wrong station too, but one of them had consulted a guidebook just before leaving the hotel, thereby avoiding the same mistake.

The more we talked, the more I came to envy the way they worked together as a traveling team. She guarded the bags while he stood in line to purchase tickets; he was in charge of planning the trip, but she held the purse strings. As darkness fell on the passing farm fields of central China, she took off her boots and he massaged her feet. The man sitting next to me was a Chinese policeman who spoke no English and didn't look inclined to rub mine.

Still, more often than not, I travel by myself even though it isn't always the most economical way to go and I know there's something silly and sad about sitting alone at a table for eight. I could claim that I do so out of necessity, because I travel so much and because for me travel isn't primarily a recreational pursuit, but a job. While many of my friends have told me they'd love to come along, I wonder how much fun they'd have doing some of the crazy things I do to get a story—like swimming with dolphins in a frigid pool in New Zealand or taking endless, uncomfortable bus rides instead of flying just to save a buck.

But the truth is, I started traveling solo many years ago on a train trip from Paris to Rome, stopping in places like Arles, where an Englishman in a cafe scolded me for being there alone in what I thought was a rather demure black dress; in Florence, where I spent one long, extremely civil afternoon drinking gin and tonics in the Piazza della Signoria with a retired American businessman, whom I never saw again; on the Ligurian Coast, where I followed the treacherous cliff path that links the villages of the Cinque Terre, dreaming dreams about Percy Bysshe Shelley; and in Rome, where I breathed exhaust fumes and dodged motor scooters on a jog from the Piazza Navona to the Colosseum. Modest adventures of a sort I could handle, but ones that wouldn't have happened in quite the same way, if I had been traveling with a companion. Ever since that trip, I've preferred solo travel.

This is above all because I get to be in control when I travel alone. I'm not so arrogant as to believe that other people don't have brilliant ideas about where to go and what to see. But I must take my own trips, find my own discoveries, make my own mistakes, and—in a way, best of all— solve them. On a camping expedition in the northern Baja with my older brother, I had no problem letting him arrange the gear, select provisions, and even plot our route because he has expertise in these areas. And when our car got stuck on a dirt road in the mountains, I was more than content to let him get it out. But I came away wondering how I'd have managed on my own. I'll never know, although I do know that when I travel with a companion I'm not as capable as I am when I'm by myself, just because I don't have to be.

Then, too, trips are precious, fragile things, easily spoiled by bad moods, sense of humor lapses, and disagreements. Even the best, most affectionate friends sometimes make uncomfortable travel companions, embarrassing each other or arguing over issues that would be of little importance at home. I wouldn't want to alienate a friend—even temporarily—over where to dine in Paris; on the other hand, I wouldn't want to give in and eat *frites* in an indifferent bistro.

A therapist might say I have control issues. Just so, and I

have other issues, as well, which compel me to behave in the alloyed ways I do. Moreover, it seems to me that travel intensifies the elements of a person's nature—both fine and toxic—making them stand out more starkly than they ever do in the safe, regulated environment of home. When I travel alone, I can give the whole mixed bag full reign, without monitoring myself, making compromises, negotiating, or even talking.

Most of all, though, when I travel solo I am somehow better able to tap my deepest thoughts and feelings. It is as if the stage clears, the background music fades, and I come forward to soliloquize. At night I dream more vividly, and during the day the stream of consciousness freely flows.

I've felt this sunning myself on Mexican beaches, wandering through the Prado, riding crowded buses in Beijing, and, above all, walking in the countryside alone. In fact, for anyone who has yearned to travel alone but felt somehow daunted, I suggest beginning with a solo walking vacation in some place that is scenically blessed but not too wild for comfort—for instance, the English Lake District, where Romantic poets like Wordsworth set a precedent for solitary rambling and musing. Henry David Thoreau tramped all over New England alone, ultimately deciding that he "never found a companion so companionable as solitude," and Robert Louis Stevenson documented a 120-mile hike he took through the mountains of southern France in *Travels with a Donkey in the Cevennes*, a plucky little book that could well serve as a primer for solo travelers.

It is important to start in a place where you feel secure, because fear is a great deterrent to solo travelers. After all, the world is hardly as safe a place as it was in the days of Wordsworth and Thoreau. This is especially true for solo budget travelers who tend to seek out edgy, low-priced destinations, take third-class buses, and frequent cheap hotels in questionable neighborhoods; solo budget travelers who also happen to be women—like me—face an even higher risk factor, or so I've read in guidebooks and brochures. As I result, I've learned to choose my destinations wisely, secure my valuables, watch where I walk, sit near the driver on overnight buses, and check the locks on hotel room doors. I've even fantasized about traveling with a pearl-handled pistol, like something Belle Starr might have tucked into her garter. And I've read with interest about the exploits of Sarah Hobson, who cropped her hair, bound her breasts, and traveled through Iran as a young man called John.

But I don't really care for guns and cross-dressing. I would rather take a cue from Stevenson, who wrote, "Something might burst in your inside any day of the week, and there would be an end of you, if you were locked into your room with three turns of the key." After all, the worst thing that ever happened to me when traveling alone was being chased by a pack of wild dogs along a jungly path on an island in the South Pacific, which had nothing to do with the fact that I'm a woman or was alone. On my own in Sophia, Bulgaria, I met a Canadian filmmaker who was so afraid of having his gear stolen that he asked if he could tour the city with me.

The dangers of traveling alone are far more subtle than robbery, rape, and murder, as far as I'm concerned. They can be summed up in a painting by Edgar Degas called *L'Absinthe*, portraying a woman alone in a Paris cafe, wearing an ugly hat and a dejected expression. She looks lonely, pitiable, and much too depressed for the Folies Bergères.

This is the way I sometimes feel, and am afraid of appearing, when I travel alone. After all, travel is an immensely romantic undertaking, leading people to think that when in Paris or Kuala Lumpur, they should be falling in love or having deep, soulful conversations with significant others. In Mexico, hotel chambermaids have searched my fingers for wedding bands, and the very fact that I was a woman traveling alone so troubled a pedicab driver on Tiananmen Square that he pinned me with as astonished glare and yelled, "Who are you? How old are you?"

Encounters like this depress me sometimes; but more often than not I am amused and touched by the varied responses I get as a woman traveling alone. By the pool at a hotel in Tahiti, a middle-aged Australian lady with a potbellied husband who'd clearly had too many Mai Tais plied me with questions about how she, too, could travel alone. Men on the make in hotel bars can't figure out why I won't let them buy me a drink. And at a four-star restaurant in Paris near the Church of St. Julien le Pauvre, the French couple at the table next to me watched me surreptitiously all through dinner—disapprovingly, I thought, until they started talking to me and wound up asking me to their apartment for drinks the next night.

I've learned a few tricks to ward off loneliness and depression, like taking care to stay healthy when away from home (because it's easy to feel blue when you start to fall ill), packing plenty of books to keep me company, and keeping photos of my family and dearest friends in my wallet. But most of all, if I start to feel low, I remind myself that I may never again get a chance to walk where Julius Caesar walked in the Roman Forum, to gaze into Lake Buttermere or see sheep climbing argan trees in southern Morocco. The place is the thing, not the way I feel. So I make a list of all the sights I've got to see, set out to visit them, and get over it.

Life is short, trips even shorter. Not wise to waste.

Let people stare and *maître d's* pretend I'm not there. Nothing will deter me.

❖ CODA ❖

HOME AGAIN

The morning I left New York in 1998, I closed the door to my apartment, went downstairs, and found a drunk sleeping in the lobby.

I took it as a sign. It was time to move on. I'd lived in the city for almost 20 years. Everyone I knew had been mugged at least once. My clothes were all black and my driver's license had expired.

I spent the next five years in L.A., mostly missing New York, especially on 9/11, when I sat on the stoop with my neighbors in Hancock Park, nursing a lighted candle, secretly feeling like a defector who could never go back to the homeland.

Then came eight glorious, nutty years abroad, writing about travel from the Seventh Arrondissment in Paris, Beijing in the run-up to the 2008 Olympics, eternal Rome in the shadow of the Coliseum.

Along the way, I rented furnished apartments, moving in with only a few suitcases. My stuff—an inadequate word for my mother's writing desk, family albums, and my college diploma—ended up in an eerie Hollywood storage unit; if I ever kill someone, that's where I'll hide the body. On visits back to L.A. I sometimes added things I'd collected on my trips: Buddhist prayer flags from Lhasa, a Vietnamese water puppet, dried lavender clipped at a friend's place in Provence. God knows what all was in there.

I found out when I finally moved back to the States and

wanted my stuff. I don't know why I returned: it just seemed like time. Or why I decided to make New York home—whatever that means—except that I'd tried all the bears' chairs and needed to sit down.

You can't come back to the United States after living abroad without sounding insufferable at dinner parties, throwing things at the talking heads on the evening news, and making endless loops through grocery stores, wondering where they keep the food. But my re-entry was easier than it might have been because New York is America's most European city, full of public spaces, less inviting to cars than to people, with history, culture, and airports—all a seven-hour flight to Paris and Rome.

But it gets better. I moved into the same building—a five-story walk-up in the West Village—where I'd lived 20 years before in a studio so small that everything had to be stowed away when not in use, as if on a boat. Back in the day, I made friends with the owner, an ex-New York City cop who'd started buying buildings in the real estate-depressed 1970s, ultimately accumulating about a dozen that he managed from an office on the ground floor. I often stopped by to discuss love and politics; he watched who I took upstairs and supported the first Gulf War.

My former landlord died while I was away, but his daughter remembered me and showed me her father's old apartment on the fifth floor, a stiff climb for a 57-year-old woman who had recently been advised to have knee replacement surgery. I looked at a couple of smaller, cheaper places on lower floors. But there was really no contest. Five C had a bedroom, kitchen, and living room, two working fireplaces, 12-foot ceilings, a big skylight, hardwood floors, a recently refitted bathroom, and three windows looking over the leafy West Village.

This is where I live now, my Rapunzel tower with four steep flights of steps instead of a witch to keep me prisoner. I do occasionally go out, and when I do, there's a new city to explore.

Its transformation started just about the time I left, as the crack cocaine epidemic wound down, helping to decrease crime almost 75 percent between 1980 and 2000. Nevertheless, on visits back, I joined an elite group of self-justifying evacuees who could afford to be nostalgic for the bad old days from a safe distance. We disdained the Magic Kingdom on Times Square, as if you earned cachet by taking your life in your hands to see a Broadway show, and claimed to prefer Astor Place without a Kmart, even if it meant having to go out to the suburbs to shop for large appliances.

I still don't like Times Square or living without a washer-dryer. While I was away, they closed St. Vincent's Hospital, a crucial fixture on Sixth Avenue that treated victims of the *Titanic*. When did bars start charging 10 bucks for a glass of house wine? And most of all, what happened to the cynicism I perfected as a New Yorker 20 years ago? It's gone out of style, along with crack cocaine and pepper spray.

I look downtown from my roof and see the new World Trade Center rising, walk west to a manicured park along the Hudson River waterfront where transvestites used to stroll, or head north on the lushly landscaped High Line, an elevated walkway on formerly abandoned elevated train tracks. And everywhere in my admittedly privileged neighborhood, flower gardens fill formerly destitute open spaces like Bleecker Street's Father Demo Square, where they've even turned on the fountain.

I'm not saying that it's morning in New York. With so many people out of work, how could it be? But there is a palpable sense of good citizenship in the city now—*civilitas,* as they say, but no longer practice, in Rome. I see the effort to do what's right in volunteers planting bulbs in Washington Square Park and, more deeply, at my favorite café, Claude's Patisserie, a buttery-smelling cubbyhole on West Fourth Street. While I was gone, Claude retired. But instead of selling out, he taught his apprentice, an immigrant from the Dominican Republic, how to make the best brioches and croissants in New York and then handed the business over to him.

I will find a style suited to New York now, but I am not sure how to be 20 years older than I was when I lived here before. I spent my 20s and 30s in the city, married, divorced, and found a métier here. I remember in those salad days of mine pitying little old ladies trying to cross Sixth Avenue in the Village before the walk light changed. On the other hand, a spry older friend of mine remarked that you'd have to go far to find an old folks' home with a Lincoln Center.

Sometimes I wonder if I will die in 5C, if the fluff 'n' fold delivery boy will smell something gnarly at my door and call the police, which happened to the old lady who lived below me in Paris. If he does, I will be found up in my tower, surrounded by the stuff that came to me in a moving van from my Hollywood storage unit: my mother's writing desk; terra cotta figurines of the Roman gods from the Italian island of Lipari; a picture of Nohant, George Sand's home in central France; and a Chinese lamp I bought at a flea market in Beijing. It took me weeks to unpack my stuff, but now it's all here. And because it is, downstairs could be anywhere.

As pleasing as I find New York now, it's a wide world out there and I'm not ready to put away my suitcases. But itinerancy no longer suits me. I want my Pakistani rug, Zulu baskets, the big oak table I bought on LaBrea Boulevard in L.A., my yellowed collection of paperback fiction by William Faulkner. Don't let ascetics tell you otherwise. Home is where the stuff is.

CREDITS

Part 1: Unforgettable

A version of "The Emerald Coast" appeared as "On Foot Along Brittany's Emerald Coast," *New York Times*, July 7, 1997.

A version of "Lost Canyons" appeared as "Exposing Utah's Depths," *Los Angeles Times*, April 3, 2005.

A version of "Sunrise at Borobudur" appeared as "In Indonesia, Watching the Sun Rise with 504 Buddhas," *Los Angeles Times*, January 6, 2012.

A version of "Across the Top of LA" appeared in the *New York Times*, June 27, 1993.

A version of "These Vagabond Shoes" appeared as "By Bus to Buenos Aires with a Soundtrack, *New York Times*, April 9, 1995.

A version of "A Bad Night's Sleep" appeared as "An Ice Place to Visit . . ." *Los Angeles Times*, February 9, 2003.

A version of "The White Horses of Wiltshire" appeared as "Tracking Wiltshire's White Horses," *New York Times*, April 4, 1988.

A version of "French Hanoi" appeared as "French Impressions," *Los Angeles Times*, May 25, 2008.

A version of "A Mexican Fish Story" appeared as "In Pursuit of the Gray Ghosts," *Los Angeles Times Magazine*, October, 10, 2004.

Part 2: Footsteps

A version of "The Two Georges" appeared as "Novel Landscapes," *Los Angeles Times*, May 8, 2005.

A version of "Colette's Ghost" appeared as "Colette's Paris," *Los Angeles Times*, May 30, 2010.

A version of "Finding Fellini" appeared in the *Los Angeles Times*, November 9, 2001.

A version of "Butch and Sundance" appeared in the *Los Angeles Times*, April 20, 2008.

A version of "The Chairman" appeared as "Understanding China Begins with a Look at Mao," *Los Angeles Times*, April 23, 2008.

A version of "Of Sword Fights and Stolen Kisses" appeared as "There's Something about Mary, Queen of Scots," *Los Angeles Times*, March 1, 2009.

A version of "Happy Endings on the Fairy Tale Road" appeared in the *Los Angeles Times*, March 18, 2001.

Part 3: Souvenirs

Versions of "My Mother's Boots" appeared in *New Woman*, September 1991, and *Making Connections* (Seal Press, 2003).

A version of "How Do You Say 'I'm Lost'?" appeared in the *Los Angeles Times*, January, 6, 2008.

A version of "The Ineluctable Allure of Lost Places" appeared as "Longing for Spots That Are No Longer on the Map," *Los Angeles Times*, December 29, 2002.

A version of "Into the Snow Globe" appeared as "Fantastical Journey: In the Frozen Winter, a Romantic Trip to St. Petersburg," *Los Angeles Times*, October 12, 2003.

A version of "On the Plateau" appeared as "Drama Along the Grand Canyon North Rim," *Los Angeles Times*, July 7, 2008.

A version of "Proust and Trader Joe's" appeared as "From Proust's Madeleine to Trader Joe's Cereal: Feeding the Hunger of Memory," *Los Angeles Times*, June 13, 1999.

A version of "Slippin' Down to the Seaside" appeared as "Freewheeling in County Clare," *New York Times*, June 16, 1996.

A version of "Cooking with Capers" appeared as "Return to Glorious Lipari," *Los Angeles Times*, February 20, 2005.

A version of "On My Own" appeared as "Two's a Crowd," *New York Times*, July 7, 1997.

A version of "Home Again" appeared as "Life Unpacked, At Long Last," *Los Angeles Times*, December 13, 2011.

ABOUT THE AUTHOR

Susan Spano has journeyed the world reporting on culture, nature, and the curiosities of humankind. She launched the still-running "Frugal Traveler" column for the *New York Times*, and later joined the staff of the *Los Angeles Times*, which sent her to the City of Light from 2003 to 2006 to start the popular travel blog "Postcards from Paris." She spent six months in Beijing studying Mandarin and researching stories in the run-up to the 2008 Olympics before moving to Rome—her favorite foreign posting—where she wrote about everything Italian, from Caravaggio to mozzarella.

Her work has appeared in the *Financial Times*, the *Chicago Tribune*, *Smithsonian magazine*, *National Geographic Traveler*, and *Redbook*; she is the co-author of *Women on Divorce: A Bedside Companion* and *Men on Divorce: The Other Side of the Story*.